HIHO

Happiness Through Self-Awareness, Intention, and Empowerment

By Cody J. Arik

Collaboration with Dr. Ernest J. Arik

Äffchen "Sir"

I dedicate this book to you, my dear friend

The are no words to convey what an honor it was to

share so much of my eternity with yours

Part of me went with you, but you gave me so much

more

You are forever part of me and in my heart

Your amazing light works though me always

Thank you

HIHO

Happiness Through Self-Awareness, Intention, and
Empowerment

Contents:

Introduction

"Life is just a 'choose your own adventure' self-help book."

"You don't throw the book away just because you made a few wrong turns. You learn from your mistakes, go back a few pages, and try again until you get it right."

– Cody J. Arik

WTF is HIHO?

H.I.H.O. stands for "Happy In, Happy Out." This idea reflects the reality of any kind of system or data: The result has a lot to do with what we intentionally put into the system. If I eat donuts, I get a net result of being less healthy. When I'm grumpy, my systems of influence give me a net result of grumpier. When I smile, I encourage smiles all around me, and the net gain is that I'm happier than I would have been without the smile.

This feedback loop doesn't occur just in the external world. I will show how learning the language your soul speaks allows you to better observe and influence the internal communication between your true self and your ego/mind. The language of the soul is often spoken in body language and facial expressions (non-verbal communication). I will introduce some basics of both, but this book is not meant to be an exhaustive resource for each aspect of body language. My intent is to give you just enough information to inspire you to pay attention to how your body language and that of others feels in the context of whatever is going on. The mere act of paying attention to things that don't seem right or in alignment can lead you to discover other possible meanings.

In addition to these feedback loops we will also look at how to have a different relationship with guilt, worry, shame, grief, and stress. And how to further grow into a person who interacts with themselves and others differently so that misery becomes a small passing curiosity.

Eckhart Tolle and Alan Watts speak wonderfully of mindfulness but do not bring in personal responsibility or morals like Jordan B. Peterson does. While Peterson does speak of the value of morals, religion, and Carl Jung's psychological shadow work, he shies away from Zen and the more metaphysical of heart-brain coherence that is common to Gregg Braden and Dr. Joe Dispenza or the overall spiritual growth and law of attraction Wayne Dyer emphasizes.

I combine the aspects of Zen, spirituality, psychology, body language, heart-brain coherence, law of attraction, and personal responsibility. This is not a book about a single topic, this is how to truly be happier for life.

Language of the Soul

I use different words throughout the book depending on which feels better, but they often mean the same thing. For example, heart, soul, inner being, true self, right brain, and higher self are interchangeable. They "think" in feelings, intuition, and emotions. They are the real you, the real self.

The mind, brain, and ego are façades and masks. They embody our more worldly desires and the parts of us that are proud and defensive, that we identify with as who we are. I will be speaking of the ego more in my second book as it's more about the nature of self, but for now I will give a brief description.

The ego is our sense of self. It is our identification with aspects of our self or our life. It is the part of us that is not only afraid to change and grow but also sees change of any kind as a type of death. The ego will fight to keep you on the same familiar path – even if it's killing you – rather than allow you to grow, change, and learn. Many spiritual teachers say we can control or eliminate the ego. Maybe

7

they are right. But in my way of thinking, the ego isn't something that can be discarded and that is a good thing. The ego is a part of our consciousness just as space-time and gravity are part of our physical world.

If you think of your mind as your house, the ego is a trickster, a gaslighting roommate you cannot evict due to local laws. At the same time it is causing this misery, it also pays the bills by helping us interact with the world and doling out rewards of pleasure and pride that keep us desiring to be kind to one another. When we strive to get rid of or control the ego, we end up being tricked (by the ego) into thinking we have indeed gotten rid of it or controlled it. We must also admit that even when we think we have learned to work with it, the ego will be telling us how cool we are for having brokered a truce between it and our higher selves. The ego is like gravity or space-time, it just is part of our reality and the best we can do is be aware that it is influencing us always. I call the ego a gaslighting, trickster, roommate we cannot evict due to local laws.

The body is also involved because it has its own ways of influencing the "system of you" through hormones and sensations. The body and the soul already know how to speak to one another and do so regularly without our conscious awareness. In this book, I will reinforce the connection of the mind to the body and soul by teaching your mind how to speak the language that the body and soul are using. The shadow and our subconscious are also part of this system, but they sit in a place between the true self and the mind. They speak with the same language as the body and soul. Only by using intentional observation can we see this communication with the conscious mind.

Carl Jung spoke of the shadow as a place in our psyche where we hide the things about ourselves we do not like and do not choose to acknowledge. These aspects of our shadow are generally unknown to us and it's very painful to uncover them. It is said that the more you need to deal with and integrate an aspect of your shadow, the more likely you will avoid it because you and especially your subconscious know it will be a painful process. We are pleasure-seeking and pain-avoidant creatures by nature, so we must remember our inclination to run and hide from that which will cause us pain, choosing instead to run toward that which gives us pleasure or be easy but may not be best for us.

Our shadow does two things: It controls us through our subconscious, and it projects those aspects of ourselves we do not like onto others. The shadow makes us see in others that which we know to be within ourselves. The less we understand our shadow, the more control it has over our lives and how we see the world and other people. That which is hidden can control us from behind the scenes, but as we work to honestly see those hidden aspects, the more control we regain over our lives and how we view the external world. I believe that learning to appreciate the pain of shadow work could easily solve 90% of our psychological issues.

Carl Jung famously said, "Everything that irritates us about others can lead us to an understanding of ourselves." At first your ego will resist and reject this concept. But as you practice seeing the "evil" of others as something within yourself, the sense of peace you gain will encourage further and enthusiastic steps into what you know will be painful because you also know that on the other side of that journey is true self-awareness and contentment like you have never known. I have reached a point where I don't get offended even though my shadow does. But more on that later...

What this Book Is, and Isn't

I am not a doctor or a psychologist and have not lived the life of either. I don't provide medical advice and happily encourage you to seek that out if you find yourself in a bad spot mentally or physically. I can only offer you the wisdom and perspective of my own experience that you can reach the same state of inner peace as I have in whatever form best suits you.

This is not a book about religion, Zen, or spirituality, but I am certainly not shy about fitting those in and offering them as ways to help. I am not religious in any traditional sense, but I encourage you to be religious if it helps you. Religious people tend to be happier than atheists because they feel part of something bigger and stable. I do consider myself "spiritual," and that the road to meaning and "something bigger" can take many forms.

I won't ask you to make lists or keep a journal like so many other books on happiness or self-improvement. You won't need them, you will simply see things differently.

I won't tell you how perfect you are now; the fact you are reading this book already suggests you know that isn't true. I also won't tell you how terrible you are, since the presence of this book in your hand indicates you are wise enough to know there is room for improvement.

This is not a motivational book and I wouldn't call myself a motivational speaker, but my ideas have had the effect of encouraging and motivating growth in those I speak to. This is a different type of book, intended to change the way you see things just enough to allow contentment to be your first and normal reaction.

If you are unwilling to look deep within yourself and make changes to your life, neither this book nor any other will be of any use to you. But if you are willing to take that journey, this book is guaranteed to improve your life and your experience of being alive.

But Why Write A Book?

I had just moved to a new city where I knew one person. I'd been laid off from my job, lost my cat "Sir" who was my best friend for 13 years, went through a divorce, and was forced to sell my home. Any of these stressful, life-changing events would have easily broken me in the past, and yet I was okay, truly okay. This is the gift I hope to give others: helping as many people as I can to feel this same inner peace in the face of any storm.

I spent most of my life very unhappy and trying to fill that hole with hedonistic and self-destructive behavior. One day I was astonished to realize that I was no longer sad or worried, I loved life. How did that happen!? I decided to find out why by deconstructing the process that had gotten me to that point. It included the knowledge of Zen, psychology, biology, body language, facial expressions, spirituality, metaphysics, law of attraction, religion, exercise, shadow work and generally a different way of seeing the world.

The process of discovering why I was no longer so sad took me down a path of much discomfort through self-reflection and admitting I was the cause of pretty much everything I didn't like about myself or my life. This is the path I will guide you on. Along the way, I may say things that offend you, but this is an opportunity to consider *why* they offend you and to reflect on what your *true* self thinks of them. I want to help you to get in the habit of questioning your life, *especially* when you're uncomfortable doing so. I found that the more discomfort I felt, the closer I got to finding my true self and with that a greater inner peace.

My interests in psychology, body language, and facial expressions gave me a unique insight into how both I and others were choosing to express ourselves and how we are hiding what we really feel. I realized our inner beings and our psychological shadows were speaking to us all the time but we refused to listen or didn't know the language. Body language is the language of the soul, the language of our shadow, subconscious, and our true, honest, inner being or soul. We are typically taught to read body language and facial expressions by looking outside at other people, but we can also learn from inside ourselves as well. And when we give a voice to that part of us, it changes how we see almost everything.

I love that I stand on the shoulders of giants. I am grateful for their brilliance and existence! I have my own way of combining concepts from different disciplines and think of myself as a bridge to and between many of these giants including Alan Watts, Eckhart Tolle, Jordan B. Peterson, Carl Jung, Dr. Joe Dispenza, Gregg Braden, Wayne Dyer, and Sadhguru. I agree with most – but not everything – they teach. The diversity of disciplines converging is quite telling, but also affirms that we as a humanity are working our collective way to an even higher truth.

I don't claim ultimate truth, but I present what I have learned and developed in the hopes of it being added to the works of these great teachers while offering a path to help you find your own truth and happiness – a truth and happiness that can help you as an individual and help you be part of raising the happiness of our collective.

I don't intend to tell you *how* to be happy, because that will come naturally as I help you remove that which is preventing an experience of true happiness that comes from your inner being. A better car won't help you get out of a traffic jam; you just need the other cars to move out of your way and clear your path.

I do intent to show you how to intentionally be happier through personal empowerment, understanding the language of your true self, and using the interconnected networks of people and influences around you. I will help you gain control of the systems and feedback loops that affect who you are and how you feel. You will come to know where and how to insert happiness into your systems of influence to improve your world as well as the worlds of those you encounter.

My dad has a great way of describing happiness: He says it's the feeling of being told "Yes." It's time to tell yourself "Yes!" to your journey to happiness.

What is Happiness?

"I have studied many philosophers and many cats. The wisdom of cats is infinitely superior."

—Hippolyte Taine

I have been blessed with a life that has taught me many wonderful and terrible things. This is how I choose to relate to the many things that have occurred in my life – usually of my doing – that I saw as maybe unfortunate at the time, but am now thankful for because they made me the person I am today.

What Is Happiness

We all want to live in a beautiful world and to feel like we are supported and loved. Fortunately, we already are in a beautiful world and are loved. We just forget to see the beauty and love for what they are and instead interpret them as misfortune and malice. Western society teaches us to want more so they can keep selling us stuff rather than seeing the support and beauty we have in abundance all around us. It can be as simple as looking for it and noticing it. The hard part is getting past the conditioning that we need more to be happy or that happiness is something to strive for. As long as you identify as striving for happiness, you always will. Instead, focus on being content and seeing the beauty all around. We always find what we are looking for, so it is up to you if you want to look for ugliness or beauty.

In the common Western vernacular, we say we want to be happier and look for ways to increase our happiness. In the Eastern philosophies, we would say we want to reduce suffering and be more detached from desire and outcomes. In both cases, what we really want is to be less miserable and more content with our current lives and what is to come. We call it "happy," but I think it's more about contentment.

Be Happy with Being Content

Happiness is an intense and wonderful feeling, certainly compared to other emotions such as anger or sadness. We want to feel happiness just like we want to feel sadness when appropriate.

Contentment is different; it's about being at peace with whatever emotions are being experienced. I use happiness and contentment interchangeably for the purposes of colloquial speech, but they are different.

Pleasure represents a temporary substitution for happiness and contentment. Too much pleasure makes it harder to feel happiness or contentment. If your house always smells like vanilla, it will be hard to notice any other fragrance. You'll also get numb to it in the same way we tend to take for granted the small things that bring joy. By all means, do that which is pleasurable, but don't think pleasure is making you content.

Like the background beat in a song, contentment can always be with you even as other emotions come and go. It becomes the baseline you return to, like your favorite warm blanket on a cold night. It's not the place you go to avoid things but rather a lens through which to view other feelings. The trick is to not get so stuck in those other emotions that contentment is not experienced. Reducing the screen time for other emotions so that contentment becomes your normal state is what I hope my words have helped you to do.

The idea of being happy all the time reminds me of *Christmas Vacation's* Clark Griswold (played by Chevy Chase) waving off the frustrations of his family during a long, bad day driving to an amusement park in the rain by saying "You'll be whistling zippity-do-da out of your assholes." This is a little too intense for my tastes.

I don't see myself as happy *all of the time*, but I will feel the emotion and then return to a baseline of lightness or contentment. A relaxed mind is not an unthinking mind; it's a mind that is free of tension. Many Zen teachings and riddles called "Koans" are designed to force you into thinking puzzles that can only be resolved by letting go. Think of a child running around all day and then passing out at the dinner table. This is what they endeavor to do to your mind in order to stop it chasing its own tail.

Over the Hill

We are often told happiness is not the point of life. This sounds honorable, but it denies who we are biologically and what motivates us. I love being happy and doing things that help me feel that way, and I suspect I am not the only one. When we look at it honestly we see that even saying, "a life of service to others is better than happiness" or "living honorably is better than happiness" are silly, because we know that doing those things gives us a type of happiness even if through pride. You are living to be happy no matter what, just decide if you want to accept the happiness directly or only accept it when it is disguised.

Where these old teachings do have it right is counseling that happiness shouldn't be a goal so much as it should be your natural state. See happiness in what is, and you always will be. There are so many things to be happy about and grateful for in everyday life. As I sit here writing at my computer, I am happy to have my cat Scribbles calmly watching me work. I am happy about the comfortable cushion where I sit to work. I love the background music that helps me concentrate. My coffee tastes great! I have electricity because I am able to pay that bill. The list goes on and on. In every moment there are plenty of things that bring happiness, and with a little practice, you will see them throughout your life as well.

We think happiness is a thing that we need to look for or wait for but it's right here, all of the time. *Seeking* happiness will cause you misery; finding happiness is about just letting yourself do so. If we think it's over the next hill, it will always be over the next hill. And if we don't see another hill right away, we will usually keep looking until we find one, or we will pile up lots of dirt to make one so we can climb it in our search. There is nothing wrong in appreciating the things that come easy when it comes to your own sense of peace.

Will you be happy once you're enlightened? If you think enlightenment will make you happy, you will keep waiting for enlightenment before you allow yourself to be happy, and that could take a very long time. And how would you know what enlightenment feels like if you have never felt it before? Maybe you will mistakenly think you're enlightened and the happiness you find will be a misunderstanding as well. Maybe the enlightenment is real, but it brings something other than happiness. Would that mean enlightenment is no longer useful or desired?

Happiness is alignment between the mind, soul, and body. This can only be increased as we become more honest with ourselves. Harmony and alignment feel good, while the disharmony from deception or false self-awareness will always lead to inner sadness. Let's get into finding that alignment ...

Alignment Practices

"In each of us there is another whom we do not know"

– Carl Jung

The mind and ego speak in words. The heart, body, subconscious, and shadow all speak in images and emotions that are expressed through body language and facial expressions. Learning to allow communication between them will help in the process of attaining true happiness.

Is this Meditation?

Before moving deeper into the message of the book, I invite you to try some alignment exercises you can use throughout your day. They will help you check in on how your mind and body are aligned with how you feel or want to feel. The focus of these simple practices is on softening the face, the importance of which will become clearer in later chapters as we discuss how your true or higher self feels. Once you get used to doing them and how they make you feel, I hope you will add them to your daily routine as they can be done anywhere at any time, such as before or during a business meeting or when you encounter a frustrating person or event and you want to realign and calm yourself.

Meditation is not natural to most and especially not to those raised in the Western world. The practices I teach are a type of meditation that will help align the heart, mind, and body but without some of the frustrations that hold us Westerners back from meditation. I realize that no one wants to be the weird person on the bus chanting "Ommm" or putting their palms face up on their knees to meditate. Most of us prefer to keep such practices personal so I keep these practices simple, subtle, and quick to do anywhere yet very effective in connecting with your inner being. But if you are willing to be more open, perhaps someone *will* notice and you will inspire them to take a moment for their own peace. Maybe it's someone who is already doing something similar and seeing you gives them the confidence to do it more. Maybe they needed a reminder and you are their sign. Perhaps you will make a new friend or just get a knowing smile.

The practices that follow are not about meditating in the traditional sense, although there are some similarities. (I highly recommend practicing meditation for the many benefits it provides.) And they don't require hours of dedicated time. Should you want to explore more traditional meditation techniques, having done these will give you a head start. If you have done more traditional meditation, I hope this adds another tool to incorporate in meditation and daily life.

I will take you first through a basic breathing practice which will lead to the full practice I have developed for learning to communicate and gain coherence between your heart and your conscious mind.

Learn the Language of Your Soul

There is the mind we all know which is our ego or our consciousness. Behind that mask is our true self. The ego communicates in words. The true self – the heart, the soul, the shadow – speaks a different language using emotions, facial expressions, and body language. If we don't listen to what it says, it will speak to us in anger, depression, and even illness. The heart needs to be heard, but we are well practiced at ignoring it. The heart and the body already speak the same language. The challenge is teaching the brain that language so there can be a more balanced alignment between heart, brain, and body.

Although not speaking the same language, the brain and body are connected. When one sends a signal, it causes a reaction in the other, which then starts a feedback loop as they look to one another for signals on how to behave or feel. For example, when your body is in a pose that implies you are ready to run away, your brain assumes that everything it perceives must be a reason you are ready to escape. When you feel sad, the muscles in your face slacken and your body takes on a similar posture. When you do something you are proud of, you stand tall and tell the world to make way for your greatness! You can also change your posture to change your mood, just as the change in mood changes your posture. When feeling sad, change it by standing up straight with your chest out and shoulders back. This tells your brain you are powerful and in control. This feedback loop and direct connection between your emotions, true self, and body is where we get body language and facial expressions. This is the language of the soul.

The following exercise can be used for your entire body, but for simplicity, I've chosen the face to start with, because it's a concentrated area where your internal emotions are displayed for you and others. It's designed to calm you and allow you to listen and learn what your true self is telling you through your facial muscles and expressions.

This first section is just about learning meditative breathing before we get to the alignment practice that involves the face and learning the language spoken by your heart and inner being. The breathing is a reminder for those already familiar with meditative practices and instructional for those who are completely new to this type of practice. This type of breathing and focus are the base of many ancient meditations.

- The eyes can be open or closed as you prefer.
- Breathe deeply through your nose into your belly. This may require some practice since we Westerners tend to breathe very shallow and into our chest. Let your belly expand as you inhale like you are trying to look pregnant. On the exhale, squeeze your belly in as if you are trying to look thinner for the cute girl walking by.
- Now bring your attention to the air as it enters and exits through your nose. Feel the air cool the skin between the nostrils as it enters. Feel how the air warms the same skin as it exits.
- Don't focus on anything except how the skin feels and the pace of your breathing. When you notice your thoughts drifting to something else, acknowledge them but don't attach to those thoughts. Gently bring your focus back to how your breath feels.

After practicing these steps just a little, you will be able to use them anytime to bring yourself back to a place of balance and alignment.

As you get more comfortable with this practice, add in the next section which will include softening of your face while being aware of the different tensions you carry there, either normally or as thoughts come and go. The intent, however, is less to soften your face than to pay attention to which feelings and thoughts influence the tension you carry there and how you truly feel about different aspects of your life. It is important to note that you will come close but will probably never succeed in fully relaxing your face because it is a direct connection to your emotions and thoughts, so it is always displaying them for us. Full relaxation is what we are working toward with the understanding that we will not get there and do not want to. Yes, I am suggesting doing something without the goal of achieving that thing – Which is a bonus lesson on Zen! This will make sense as you practice it. You will get close, but where your tension returns is something you will come to appreciate knowing.

See your Face in the Mirror of Your Mind

It's important to feel what our face is doing and recognize how that is tied to the thoughts we have and to the feelings of our inner being. This next practice is also simple, but brings a lot of learning and awareness. You can do it for as long as you are comfortable; you will learn as much as you notice and are honest about.

- As with the previous exercise, your eyes can be open or closed but closed may help you focus at first.
- You won't need to pay as much attention to the breath but keeping it deep and regular is great for focus.
- Flex all of the muscles in your face, not all at once, just move everything around a bit to loosen it all up. Side to side, up and down. Flex and stretch everything from the forehead, to the nose and cheeks, to the lips and jaw. Just make sure everything moves as this will break loose the features we hold tight by habit.
- Now relax and soften your face. I like to imagine my facial features more rounded and without expression – neutral without judgement, like a puppy who has exhausted himself with play and is resting peacefully or the face of a cat kneading a blanket before settling down on it.

- When your face is soft and relaxed, it sends a signal to the brain that everything is okay. (If things were not okay, your face would be contorted or tense.) This is the first milestone of this practice: using your facial muscles to communicate to your mind that you are fine. This alone can bring your mindset to a more peaceful state and can through feedback help you drop any troubling thoughts that are causing tension.

- Now do a mental scan of the muscles in your face and feel for areas of tension. Where you tend to hold tension can sometimes be visible in the form of wrinkles (e.g., the forehead). I have reduced the number and severity of wrinkles on my face by teaching my facial muscles to relax and using this mind/muscle feedback loop to create a stronger sense of inner peace. (looking younger is another benefit)

- Relax each point of tension as you notice it. Don't be frustrated if the tension comes back; that is useful information and this process takes time. Just let it relax or flex or stretch the tense muscle and then let it go. Areas of tension can mask other tensions so as you let one go, you may notice other tight spots.

- Work your way to each part of the face several times: your forehead, brow, temples, eyes, nose, cheeks, tongue, jaw, lips, neck, – even the muscles on the top of your head or behind your ears pulling on your face.

- Don't worry about forcing your thoughts in a particular direction or trying to stop them. When a thought pulls you away from your focus, recognize what it is, let it pass, and return your focus to relaxing your facial muscles. The intent is learning about the relationship between your thoughts and feelings and where and how they show up on your face.

- As you focus on the muscles in your face, start to notice your thoughts when you sense a facial muscle tighten. Did you think of something that angers you? What muscles tightened for anger? The same goes for any emotion: frustration, sadness, joy, love – even something that doesn't feel "right" or out of alignment with your true self. This will be a learning process of noticing the correlation between the thought and the muscles. As you release one tense spot, a new thought will form, more tension will show up, you will notice that emotion, and release that tension as well. You are learning to read your own facial expressions that generally go unnoticed or at least unacknowledged and underappreciated. I like to think of it as seeing my face in the mirror of my attention.

And by the way, the connection goes both ways. Purposely tensing areas of the face can also cause you to feel certain emotions or bring up thoughts associated with the emotion that correlates with the tension. For example, squeezing the brow can make you feel and think of angry things. Raising your eyebrows, tightening your brow, and opening your eyes wide can cause you to feel worried or concerned. Pulling your lips tight can make you feel like you are holding yourself back or hiding something. Letting your cheeks drop creates feelings of guilt or sadness. Raising both corners of your mouth feels peaceful and happy. While raising just a single corner feels devious. When you tense a part of your face, does it produce a thought or memory along with the emotion? That is something to notice and use for further investigation into who your higher self is or wants to be.

Here are some variations to this exercise that will broaden your perspective and self-awareness:

- Notice how your body is physically positioned; those postures are also part of the feedback system between the brain and body. I only suggest starting with the face because it's a concentrated area with unlimited information about how we feel and what affects us. The same principle works with body postures. You will see, for example, that standing up straight makes you feel more in control while hunching over feels powerless and scared.

- Try asking your heart how it feels about something while doing this practice. Think of something happy and notice how your face relaxes as the corners of the mouth turn up and the areas around the eyes slightly tense. Think of something sad and you will feel your cheeks sag as the mouth turns down. I like to think of my cat to calibrate what happiness and love feel like. You may use anything such as a child or a favorite memory to calibrate love or anything that has a familiar associated feeling for you. Take it a little further and think of a belief you have or a choice you want to make.

- You can also program yourself using this. Maybe you have a coming meeting or conversation that is causing you stress. In this state where your facial muscles are relaxed and you are in a feedback loop of no stress, think of that event. Allow yourself to think through how the conversations may go, even as you think of the worst case, allow a subtle smile on your face, slightly pull up the corners of your mouth and tighten the muscles around your eyes. This teaches your subconscious this event is associated with peace rather than fear. It can go the other way too, think of a food or habit you do not prefer, then let the corners of your mouth drop in a frown or make an asymmetrical face of disgust as if you smelled old garbage. This associates whatever it was in a way that makes you not desire it as strongly.

There will be times when you have relaxed a part of your face and it feels as if the tension is gone. If you do another scan, you may find that the tension has moved to another area. This is why I invite you to practice this exercise frequently as it teaches you to notice the tension, appreciate it, and let it go. A relaxed face indicates to your mind that there are no worries, there is nothing to fear. Part of being happy is noticing when you aren't aligned and then taking steps to get back to center. Being happy and content is natural; we just need to keep reminding ourselves of that.

Learning this skill will make it easier to add more steps that include the entire body – its poses and postures – and bring greater focus to what it feels like to be out of alignment. It will also teach you how to read the body language of others as you learn what "tension in context" looks like while you are communicating with them.

This practice will also help you to align your mind, body, and true self with the added benefit of teaching yourself body language and facial expression reading. As you gain comfort with this practice, you will start recognizing your true feelings during events or conversations. You will also notice that you have learned to read the body language of others and the shadow language of both yourself and those you encounter.

Your ego and conscious mind may have some opinions on the benefits of these practices based on logic or fear, but don't let them derail you. The true self will speak to you through these shifts in the muscles of your face and the muscles and postures of your body.

I invite you to pause here and take another moment to soften your face and make listening to your soul a habit.

Breathe Your Intentions

This alignment exercise is very easy and can be done anywhere for whatever length of time you like. I like to do it for just a couple breaths, which only takes a few seconds.

- Eyes open or closed as your preference and situation allow.
- Breathe deep into your belly through your nose.
- Feel the cool air as it enters your nose.
- As that fresh air comes in, think of a positive word or two that represent what you are in need of at the moment. Some examples:
  - Peace
  - Love
  - Calm
  - Courage
  - Patience
- Think of what that word means to you as you feel it filling your lungs and body.
- As you exhale and relax, think of the word "release" but don't release anything in particular – just experience the sensations of releasing, relaxing, and letting go.

[Some practices use the exhale to let go of something negative, but I advise against that because the mind likes to grab onto negative thoughts and run with them. I prefer to focus on what I want to feel, not what I don't want to feel.]

Accept a Gift

When you feel as if something is missing in your life or you are experiencing an unfulfilled desire, accept it as a gift.

Close your eyes and extend a hand in front of you with your palm up and imagine something being placed in it. It can be anything: a specific item or a feeling of love or acceptance – whatever feels appropriately meaningful to you. A symbol for confidence could be the face of a person from history or your life whom you admire. Perhaps you need the comfort of a cup of hot chocolate. A feeling could be a shape if that is what your mind settles on. Allow yourself to come up with whatever represents the gift you are receiving.

Once you imagine the "item" being placed in your hand, gently close your fingers around it and bring it to your heart to indicate that you have truly accepted the gift. I like to open my hand as I place it and the visualized image on the center of my chest.

Be as calm or excited about your gift as you like –
whatever feeling helps you make the experience real. It's
your gift and your feeling! Your soul will feel the gift is
genuine and was received with love.

Go with a Smile

Practice smiling without intent or reason. A soft, subtle,
peaceful smile you give to an awkward clump of grass you
walk past just as willingly as you offer to a person you find
beautiful. This is not something we are used to doing, as you
can tell by the number of people you pass with grumpy
faces.

To begin, choose something simple and pleasant to start
practicing with. I recommend a flower, but it can be
anything that gives you a sense of calm and peace,
something that can't judge you or think you strange for
staring. Look at this flower (or whatever you choose) and let
the corners of your mouth gently raise as you feel the peace
and joy it brings just for existing. Just appreciate it for being
it and smile.

Having mastered that, go for a walk, in or out of your
house, and smile the same way at everything you pass: a
tree, a chair, the sidewalk, a fence, a passing car, a child, a
cat. Appreciate them for existing. Consider what got them

there. Think of how much joy they provide. Think of how lucky you are to see this beauty that most people ignore.

Now you are ready for adults! Smile at everyone for no reason, not because they are pretty or did something funny. Just smile with the same calm, peaceful smile you looked at the flower with. Not to impress or attract them; not even to start a conversation. People can tell when you have intent, and it can feel creepy or unsettling. Just appreciate them as you pass.

When you do this without intent, they will know your appreciation is pure and they will usually give you a smile in return, increasing the joy in even the most potentially unpleasant interactions. How do you want others to feel? Grumpy or filled with peace and love?

Keep up this habit. Make smiling your normal and you will give and attract happiness wherever you go!

Being a Better Person

"Many are stubborn in pursuit of the path they have chosen, few in pursuit of the goal."

--Friedrich Nietzsche

Spoiler Alert: You are already a better person than you think you are!

Do you ever wonder if you are a good person? If you do, then you are, at least to the best you can understand what that means.

Look in Your Hand

Did a horrible and mean person pick up this book to stop being horrible and mean? Why would a horrible and mean person even do such a thing? If you think you're a terrible person, you must be good enough to tell the difference between good and bad. Maybe you tell yourself you are useless. How many useless people would want to read a self-help book that would make them more useful? Wouldn't they already be useful for no longer wanting to be useless?

The fact that you want to be a better person means you are already that person and your ego has not kept up with that knowledge. Why would anyone but a better person want to read a book that has the intent of helping them along the path to being better? Now if we already think we're good, we can lose the motivation to do more, but most people who are good at heart always want to improve themselves and serve the world.

If you consider yourself too awesome, you will overlook your flaws. If you see yourself as horrible, you will overlook all your fantastic attributes.

I avoid telling people "You are perfect just the way you are," just as I avoid telling people they need to be something different. If I do either, I am saying that you shouldn't become what your potential allows. Or I'm telling you that who you have grown into isn't good. I may tell you that something you did was great or that you acted in a spectacular or horrible way, but I avoid telling people what they are, just as I try to avoid defining myself as perfect *or* in need of work.

Gautama Buddha grew up as a prince who was given the best possible life of wealth and comfort that he rejected. In becoming an icon for enlightenment, he showed that suffering isn't mandatory and that we keep growing because each enlightenment is just a step to the next enlightenment. He forced suffering upon himself, but later learned the suffering wasn't necessary.

The story goes that he and his followers sat under a Bodhi tree for many days without food or personal care in an attempt to understand the secret of enlightenment. One day a young woman brought Buddha a bowl of rice. He ate the rice, then got up and bathed himself. It was then he decided that suffering wasn't necessary and invited his followers to come with him on a different path. But when he walked away from the Bodhi tree, his followers abandoned him because they had become so identified with suffering that their egos would not let them be happy or see the lessons and values that happiness can bring. They were so caught up in trying to *be* better people that they forgot to allow themselves to *grow* into better people.

Be Your Own Baseline

What is a better person? Is it someone who wants to do kind acts for others and make the world a better place? A person who makes a lot of money or does a great job taking care of their own needs? Does a good person walk their dog more often?

How do you know what makes a good person? Listening to what someone else tells you? Looking at others as examples of what a good person is? Both are great places to learn, but what really matters is figuring out for yourself what makes you a good person.

If you told a Zen master that you wanted to be a better person, they would ask why you want that. You may tell them so you can like yourself more, but they might wonder why someone not worthy of already liking themselves would even know what that means.

They may then ask you what "better" is. When you tell them it's someone who does more good deeds in the world, they may give you a blank stare, as if to ask, "Why are you sitting here in the temple if you want to be out doing good in the world?" If you are so aware of what needs to be done, nobody is stopping you from doing it!

A priest may tell you to do as Christ would do. But you can only know what Christ would do up to your understanding of what the good of Christ is, put another way, as you are allowing that essence to come through you. A priest may point out a direction and be someone to talk to, but your "Christ within" is sitting on hold, waiting for *you*.

Again, you can only be as good as your capacity to recognize and understand what better means. If you can point to any action and say it's better, then you understand it and can reach for it. Someone who is addicted to alcohol or drugs won't care about kicking the habit until they decide a better person is someone who does not take drugs.

Psychopaths and saints each have very different ideas about what being a better person is, and to themselves, they aren't wrong. To each, the actions needed to be that better person will support their version of happiness. The same is true or you. Your version of what better is will do a lot more to lead you to happiness than any version given to you by others. Since this book is about *your* personal happiness, I will do my best to avoid telling you that vanilla tastes better than chocolate.

Do you get offended?

"Everything that irritates us about others can lead us to an understanding of ourselves" – Carl Jung

When you get offended, that is not you, it is your ego and shadow that get offended.

When someone says something that offends you:

- What they said was false, so they are not speaking to or about you, they are speaking of a fictional character in their mind. They are creating a strawman or icon of you so they can punch it. They are not punching you. There is no reason to be offended. Like someone calling you a 'shower curtain' if you are not that thing, their words have no power and seem unworthy of response.

- What they said is correct and is something that you like about yourself or are proud of. In this case also there is no need to be offended. Say you are a proud landscape painter, when someone uses "artist' as an insult, it has not weight effect but to compliment you.

- What upset you is something you know to be true and you do not like about yourself. Getting offended does not fix the issue, better to appreciate the reminder of where you have opportunities to grow as a person. Being offended only gives you an excuse to limit yourself and avoid the work to grow.

- This is the one that sucks but is by far the most useful. What they said is true and is something you do not know or like about yourself, something you are not aware of that has been hidden in your shadow. The trick here is to notice you are pointing the finger outward, then to fight everything your ego tells you and force the direction of the pointing inward instead. I can promise this will not come easily or naturally. Like above; this is a place where you can choose to be grateful but even more so because this is something you were not previously aware of that has been shown to you. Something you can recognize and admit which allows you to grow. You can't fix what you do not know about, so indeed you have been given a gift. When you do uncover something you did not know was in your shadow, you can now accept it as something you like about yourself or you can recognize it as something to work on changing. You can continue to be offended or you can rise above and use that feeling as a signal to grow. And again, we see there is no need to be offended.

To recap and simplify: When someone upsets you, pause and look inward to see where you can grow before assuming the problem is them. Most often, what we see in them is a reflection or projection of who we are rather than who they really are. When you do get offended remember what you are saying is "It is easier and hurts less for me to blame you than to do the work of investigating and uncovering a flaw I have."

When you are offended take it internally and recognize it as a problem within yourself. You can then choose to move it to something you like about yourself or something you do not like about yourself and want to work to resolve. In either case there is no need to be offended, you have grown and integrated a part of your shadow that had previously been controlling you through your subconscious.

This is a hard pill to swallow but once you get it down, you will start to appreciate where you are shown opportunities to grow and you will honestly see the difference between your projections of self onto others and their true nature. You must first learn to love seeing the negative about yourself, in yourself or reflected in others, and making it a first reaction to ask how that is your issue. It is easy to say it is their problem or their behavior, but there is no personal growth when it is 'them'. Recognizing the future peace and contentment that come from accepting or fixing an aspect of yourself is a far greater feeling than shifting the responsibility to the person you are projecting that negative aspect of yourself onto. You have the ability to fix one person, their name is on your birth certificate.

The Golden Shadow

The Golden Buddha is a well-known statue located in the temple of Wat Traimit in Bangkok with an interesting story. In 1957, it was being transported to a new temple. It was dropped, cracking some of the plaster and revealing what was underneath – gold. Apparently, it had been covered in plaster and broken bits of colored glass centuries earlier to protect it from invaders who would do it harm. Sound familiar? We all resemble this golden buddha in that we each have a shining golden aspect that we have done an exceptional job covering up with metaphorical plaster. We have done this to protect ourselves from the potential emotional pain, from being laughed at, and being seen as weak. To our ego this is the same as being attacked physically.

C.G. Jung spoke of "the shadow" where all the things we don't like about ourselves are hidden. There is also a shadow where we put all the wonderful things about ourselves. Just as Jung's idea of the psychological shadow projects our denied and negative aspects onto other people, the golden shadow projects wonderful things about ourselves onto others in the form of idolizing them or thinking you could never be as good as them.

The golden shadow may have kindness because at some point our expression of it was used against us. Love and trust may be there as well because in the past they made us vulnerable and we were hurt. That we can recognize these traits in others means we have them ourselves, so when I

47

idolize someone for being generous, it's because that impulse is also in me trying to get out. I would not even know to idolize generosity if I weren't already capable of it, I might instead see it as a form of weakness.

Who do you admire? Why do you admire them? You only know to admire someone based on your capacity to understand the good they are doing. You have permission to work toward being like anyone you admire!

Which Delusion Do You Prefer?

There is a story of a master and his student often taught in martial arts called "The Warrior in the Garden":

The student asks the master, "How can you teach fighting and killing techniques yet also teach and practice peace?"

The master replies, "It is better to be a warrior in a garden than a gardener in a war."

The gardener in a war can barely keep himself alive. The warrior in the garden can take care of himself on the battlefield, and when working in a garden, with leftover capacity to help others.

In modern times we live in a metaphorical garden where everything is easy and abundant to the point that we have forgotten many of the aspects of personal responsibility and what is truly important. We have also forgotten to feel gratitude for everything around us and have come to feel entitled to it. Most of us would be so out of place in a harsher environment that we would not survive a day yet we complain at the slightest inconvenience. Take for example complaining the internet is slow rather than marveling what a wonderful tool we have even on its worst days. We can choose to be simple gardeners who only tend our own fields and help others when it's easy, blaming the success or failure of our fields on something outside us like the weather, other people, or the government. Or we can become like warriors: strong and capable, taking responsibility for our actions or inactions, accepting both our failures and our greatness. One cannot truly accept their successes until they also accept responsibility for their failures, it is either you causing all events in your life or you are powerless. Each event you say was the fault of something external gives your power away and each event you (good or bad) you take responsibility for increases your personal power. Accept the pain of being at fault for everything so that you can truly feel the pride and joy of being the agent of your own successes. When you point at what is stopping you or holding you back, that is what you give your power to, I would suggest pointing at yourself as being the cause of your issues as often as possible in order to keep that divine power.

We are each the warrior or the gardener in different situations. To some, for example, standing up to their boss is easy, while to another it may be something from their nightmares. Know where in life you are a warrior and where you are a gardener so that you can improve, help, or plan accordingly.

The definition of a storm is different for each person. Did that wind blow me around or was I ill-prepared for it? A hurricane to a gardener may be a gentle breeze to a warrior. Why would they each see it differently? Is one of them delusional? Which delusion would you rather have?

I choose to enjoy the gentle breeze in the middle of a hurricane.

Make Life as Hard as You Need it

Some people like to say and or feel that they've had a hard life and there are usually reasons for why they feel that way. But comparing my life to yours reveals nothing except that we both have egos. To each their burden is heavy, so we can all say we have had hard lives and we can all be correct in making that statement for ourselves.

We often think that to attain some sort of enlightenment or progression in life that we must go through hard times. And to anyone who believes this, I recommend that you keep going through those hard times until you no longer see their value. Hard times can absolutely be a way to force a lesson that we may not otherwise learn. The danger is assuming it's the only way to learn. Ask yourself: "How much suffering is necessary for what level of enlightenment?" See what I mean? If you are going to claim suffering is necessary, then you should be able to quantify it.

We can certainly be grateful for the lessons that come from hard times, just as we can be grateful for the lessons from easy times. Unfortunately, we often forget the latter. The phrase "This too shall pass" is commonly used when going through hard times but is forgotten when going through good and easy times. It is just as true for both. Learning to be grateful for as much as possible in any moment can make it easier to move back and forth between hard and easy times.

While going through the worst of times, ask yourself; "what am I learning that can make the time feel valuable?". We cannot always see the lesson until the hard times have passed, but asking the question and looking for the positive can take the edge off feelings of doom and make you feel more in control. During the best of times, ask yourself; "Am I showing gratitude for everything I have?". It's easy to take good things for granted and forget how wonderful it is to have them. Answering both of these questions will help make you stronger and prouder of yourself.

The best self you can imagine is your higher self, and it is always accessible to you. Perhaps you fall short due to fear or shame or simply a lack of practice but it is in you. Falling short or raising the bar are both great because you always have something to strive for. Give yourself permission to be as good as your capacity allows and to increase that capacity so that you have permission to move even further in a positive direction.

Systems of Influence

"A human being is a part of the whole called by us universe, a part limited in time and space. He experiences himself, his thoughts and feeling as something separated from the rest, a kind of optical delusion of his consciousness. This delusion is a kind of prison for us, restricting us to our personal desires and to affection for a few persons nearest to us. Our task must be to free ourselves from this prison by widening our circle of compassion to embrace all living creatures and the whole of nature in its beauty."

- Albert Einstein

Our lives – and the communities we live in – are rooted in interconnected and intertwined systems, circles, and feedback loops of influence. As part of these circles or systems, what we put into them affects us emotionally, mentally, and even spiritually.

What are Systems of Influence?

These feedback loops can be the people (and pets) within your house, your job, your neighborhood, your city, your country. The traffic around you, everyone at the grocery store, even someone you walk past on the street. Each of these will have different levels of effect on you and your life, just as your effect on them will vary by the size of the circle of impact and length of interaction. The smaller the circle, the more powerful the effect because the reverberation will be faster and stronger. You as an individual are the smallest but most powerful feedback loop.

We spend our days in any number of these circles at any given time, entering and exiting them as fluidly as our life moves. Learning to recognize your circles of influence as you are in them helps you feel more in control – if they are invisible, your options for control are reduced.

Each person you interact with is part of your circle, but they are also part of other circles. The checker at the grocery store I talk to is part of my circle at that moment and part of the circle that consists of everyone in the store. And we each have our own circles of friends and family that are separate systems we influence and are influenced by. If I am unpleasant to the checker, I'm doing a lot more than being mean just to them, that unpleasantness ripples. I am inserting it into my current circle and making my own day worse. I am inserting this energy into the systems of everyone around within earshot. I am making this checker's day a little worse which they may then take to their family or friends. All of this connects to the much larger circle that is my town. When I walk down the street, for example, and nobody is smiling, it can feel sad and isolating. How I am at least in part to blame for this? When enough people shift their attitudes, they shift the culture of their town.

Interconnected Systems of Influence:
How do these systems connect to and influence one another?

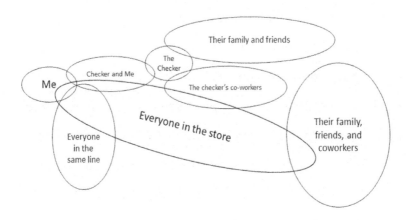

You can see above that each circle or system connects to many others.
Each affects, influences, and feeds back into those touched directly or indirectly.

A feedback loop happens when any new element is inserted into a system. I like to think of this as like a conference call where two people in a room have their speakers and microphones on. If someone enters the room and says "Hello," it can echo from speaker to microphone over and over until it becomes a loud and reverberating "whawhawhawha" sound.

Anyone who deals with looking at data knows this in another way: "Garbage in, Garbage out." The quality of your output from your data or system will be equal to the quality of the data you put into it.

The same principles apply to any kind of energy we put out in the world, negative or positive. So why not choose to put a smile into the system? Having a less than stellar day? Wouldn't a smile from someone make that sad day just a little more awesome? Insert into the system that which you wish to get out of it.

When you smile at the person walking past you, chances are they will smile back. You just got smiled at. WIN! They became your agent of happiness and you used their smile to make your day better. And hopefully as a side effect, you just made their day better as well. Maybe they go home and give their kids an extra smile. Their kids go to school the next day and maybe one of them smiles at *your* child, who then brings an extra smile home with them. Maybe they do not smile back, so what, you still put one more smile into your personal system of influence.

I'm not saying a smile given to a co-worker or stranger will suddenly mean world peace, but it is guaranteed to counter something negative that was put into the world and will certainly counter something negative that was in *your* world. I encourage you to be self-centered and greedy about your happiness!

The Unintentional are Unknowing Agents of the Intentional

Intentional actions have far more power than unintentional ones. When I choose to pick something up, there is a far greater chance it will end up in my hand than if I wait for it to get there some other way.

None of these systems are closed and you shouldn't think of them that way or you'll get frustrated. Because each system is getting input from all the other systems and circles of influence, it's the intention that matters most. There is no way you or I can control what external circles are doing or what is put into them before they interact with our direct circles, and fortunately, we don't need to. We can do just as well in the world by focusing on ourselves and those around us.

I'm nice to the family dog, which makes both the dog and I happier.

The now happier dog hangs out with my spouse making them happier.

Later my spouse and I spend time together.

Because I put more happiness into the system that is me and my dog, I improved the dog's happiness as well as my own. This later led to my spouse and I having increased happiness.

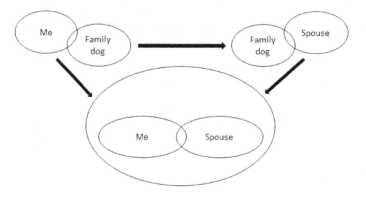

I did something for myself, which was playing with the dog and having fun.

This later fed back to me to further increase my happiness.

The side effect was increasing the happiness of the dog and my spouse.

Without a doubt, negative influences outside of you can affect you and the circles you are directly and indirectly connected to. They are not competing with you, though; they simply exist and will do what they will do. Those negative effects usually have no specific intention to harm so they will have less power than your own intentional influences. Someone who got in a fight with their boss could, in their anger, cut you off in traffic. They don't intend to ruin your day, but their action may still impact you. However, if you've already been putting intentional happiness into your system, you may get annoyed or be affected but you will still come out ahead. Had you not been feeding into your loop intentionally with positive energy, you would be more vulnerable. But you did, and the jerk on the road will have much less power. The goal is to create a net positive effect in your life and on your happiness with your intentions, choices, and behaviors. Remember: what we seek is a "net positive" effect, even just a tiny bit better each day compounds into something wonderful over time.

When a group is deciding where to eat, it's usually the person with the strongest intention who gets everyone to go along with what they want. If your intention to be good is stronger than the intention of someone being bad, think how much of a positive impact you can have!

Watching protests, situations become violent because people lose their intent to keep things civil and organized. All it can take for chaos to explode is for one person with strong intent to start damaging property who then influences those with weak intent to join the party. Should you find yourself in such a situation, hopefully you have firmly set your intent ahead of time so you can be an agent of order and reason helping prevent peaceful events from becoming violent ones.

H.I.H.O.

As I mentioned above, system inputs influence system outputs. That's why I like the idea of "HiHo": "Happy in, Happy out." Just like putting garbage into a system results in garbage as the output, intentionally putting even a little more happiness into the world results in greater happiness as the net result for yourself and others.

I like the acronym 'HiHo' because it first has the effect of releasing a little steam by doing what you want and calling the person (or situation) a 'Ho' in your head. Let's be honest, you were going to do something similar anyway. Now that the pressure is let out a little, you can use HiHo as a reminder that you are in control of the intention you put back into whatever system you happen to be in. I can *choose* to make a person an agent of my intention or at least refuse to pass someone's negativity along to others. If I happen to improve the day and attitude of an angry person, my win gets even bigger. Most important is that I do not propagate the negative, replacing it instead with happiness, joy, and love.

Does the coworker who always talks about how horrible everything is help you get through the day with a lighter step? Maybe you can turn some of their comments around and point out evidence to the contrary. Demonstrate to them and to yourself that being positive feels better and can be normal.

When my work environment is less than perfect, I can either be a victim of that negative culture or empower myself to make it as good for myself and others as is possible from my position. If my work happiness is 4 on a scale of 1 – 10, I may not be able to reach 10 by smiling at someone, but my daily efforts to always smile at and be pleasant to those around me *will* have subtle, positive effects. Maybe they will slightly improve the days of those near me, who then take that energy home and are more upbeat with their family that night. The next day at work they may smile a little bigger when we say "Hello." Now my new day is brighter as this slight shift passes around the office and maybe we go all from a 4 to a 5 in happiness. Like a snowball rolling down a hill, it's bound to pick up size and momentum.

When you see what a negative attitude can do to those around you (and, if you could, those they then interact with), you probably do not want to "be that person" who is responsible for making the days of distantly influenced people a little less happy. We also want to be careful of what we choose to echo back and into those around us. If someone is being a jerk, for example, I can choose to be a jerk to the next person or smile and give them a compliment to neutralize the negative that was given to me.

If someone cuts you off on the road, give someone else the opposite: extra room or time for their lane change. This will help counter that negative and normalize kindness. Most importantly, you remind yourself and reinforce your view of yourself as a good, honorable, and kind person, that feels good and increases your happiness.

The most powerful feedback loop you can be in is the one that is inside you. Since the smaller the circle, the more potent the effects, I suggest you be as kind to yourself as possible. This means smile at yourself in a mirror, compliment yourself instead of criticizing, sit or stand straight and proud, and always think of the best-case scenarios. You can only think one thought at a time, so whatever you focus on becomes feedback into the system of you. When you catch yourself thinking a negative thought, replace it with a more positive one. This does take practice. Think of how long you've practiced thinking negative thoughts – and look at how good most of us have become at that! You can get just as good at thinking positive thoughts.

Smile for a Smile

Be nice to people and make heaven a place on earth or a kingdom within. Take some time to review your life and notice the pain you may have caused others as well as the joy of those you've helped. If you feel you've caused more pain than joy, you have the rest of your life to balance it out and then some.

It can't be over-emphasized: When you smile at people, they will naturally smile back, which makes your world and theirs that much brighter. When you smile at someone and they smile back, allow your imagination to think of all the ways you might have contributed to making their life better. Maybe it was a bad day and you showed them that there is love in the world and they took that with them and made their family better or their workplace better. Maybe it wasn't even them who needed the smile but the cashier at the store. When you smiled at them, they took that smile and shared it with that cashier.

By smiling at each other, you both may end up smiling at the next person and then the next person, and then they smile at someone else, and so it goes. You can get smiles all day long simply by putting it out to the world in your own small, honest, and subtle way that it's okay to smile. When you look at somebody walking down the street, think about a friend you love and smile at them like you're seeing your friend – or a new friend. If they don't smile back, be sympathetic that they haven't yet reached that part of their journey and maybe don't even know they are on a journey. How could you not be happy and grateful in a world where so many people are smiling at you?

Lying to Ourselves

"Above all, don't lie to yourself. The man who lies to himself and listens to his own lie comes to such a point that he cannot distinguish the truth within him, or around him, and so loses all respect for himself and for others. And having no respect he ceases to love, and in order to occupy and distract himself without love he gives way to passions and coarse pleasures, and sinks to bestiality in his vices, all from continual lying to other men and to himself."

—Fyodor Dostoyevsky (*The Brothers Karamazov*)

We often do not notice when we lie to ourselves; it has become that normalized. We simply assume that uncomfortable feeling in the back of our minds is what thinking sometimes feels like. Lying to the most important person in your world – you – makes lying to others and being lied to that much easier. Lying is intentionally giving up a small piece of your soul in trade for a personal payoff or reward.

How do we Lie to Ourselves?

We lie to ourselves to fit in. We lie about our morals, our beliefs, our likes and dislikes, what we want, and so many other things. We may not consciously recognize ourselves doing this, but our subconscious knows, our hearts know, our true selves know when we are deceiving ourselves. Each time we aren't honest with our true selves, we erode our soul and sense of self-worth just a little. Whether we lie intentionally or not, we are telling ourselves we are the type of person who lies, lowering the respect we have for ourselves. Since we are ourselves people, we are saying it's okay to lie to people in general. That means we are also telling ourselves, as people, it is ok for us to be lied to, opening us up to accepting lies from others. It is up to you to decide if the lie is worth that price.

The unity of our thoughts and actions with our true self feels comfortable, like a freshly paved road. There's a feeling of lightness and happiness that leads to a more general sense of well-being. Disharmony from our inner self is like a bumpy and rutted country road. There is neither flow nor peace. And because we've become so used to it, we don't often know it is disharmony we feel or lying that we are doing. The challenge is learning to feel the difference between unity and disharmony. That is what the Alignment

Practices chapter at the start of the book is intended to help you decipher.

Lies can feel good at first, but their effect goes far deeper and is far more disruptive. This applies to intentional lies, little white lies, and unintentional lies that go against the beliefs and morals of our true selves. It's like taking alcohol, drugs, or anything that numbs a pain; it may disguise that pain for a while, but under the surface it's there and growing and becoming much more of a monster that you will have to contend with later.

Consider the lies you tell to other people, if you truly care about the other people then you would not want to create a monster within them that grows and become something more vicious that they will have to deal with later, if you truly care about other people you would want to remove those monsters for them to allow them to be more their true selves in a more honest world. When we lie to others we normalize lying in general and we normalize thinking that particular lie as a truth or something they too can lie about.

Both our inner being and our shadow have their own languages. When our inner being sees that something is out of alignment, it speaks to us in emotions and feelings of anger, offense, and discomfort. Our shadow, the repository of everything we don't like about ourselves, will project those traits onto others and sabotage our capacity for connection and compassion, that is its language.

In addition to the above ways of speaking to us, our true self, subconscious, and our shadow want to get out and be expressed and can speak through body language and facial expressions. When a true self is being repressed, you can sometimes see it in a person's facial expressions and physical motions. It can be the look of a hostage begging with their eyes to be released or an excited, happy, child doing their favorite activity. There is something intense and terrifying or even ecstatic and wonderful when that controlled or captive person breaks through their mask to reveal that normally hidden self. It depends on what aspect is being revealed from behind the mask, is it their higher self's passion or is it something terrible from their shadow.

The best example I can use of a shadow aspect is the character of Bilbo in Tolkien's *Lord of the Rings* trilogy. A humble hobbit, Bilbo is in seeming control of his faculties until he desires for the "ring of power," which reveals that evil hidden part of him. The ring takes over and for that brief time the mask slipped and his shadow's desires were revealed. He went from a calm old man to an angry hateful creature.

When it is a positive aspect of their true self, you can see the person almost revert to their childhood as they excitedly tell you about their love of art, trains, skiing, or hiking gear. The reserved adult you were speaking with vanishes and is replaced with this happy and passionate soul.

You will learn to feel this inner captive as you start watching for it in yourself and others. When observing others, the first step is paying attention to what is being said when you notice a change in their behavior. From there you will learn how to translate that information and become more willing to notice it within yourself. I again invite you to return to the chapter on Alignment Practices at the start of the book if you have not become familiar with the language of your soul and the exercise to learn it.

What is holding your true self hostage? Fear. The fear of being pushed away by your group, of making a change, and worst of all, of realizing you have been deceiving yourself. When you lie to yourself, you become your own hostage and make yourself a slave to those lies. It can be hard to change course because to stop lying to yourself, you must first admit you've been doing it, and who wants to admit they've been tricked? You cannot break chains you don't know you have. But by paying close attention and being open to truth, you will break them.

Let your inner hostage free and help others free theirs by allowing and normalizing honesty in yourself and those around you. You'll make yourself happier both directly and because of the elevated happiness of those around you who have permission to speak from their heart.

The Shadow

C. G. Jung wrote a lot about "the shadow" and I give you a short summary for the purposes of this book.

As I mentioned earlier, our psychological shadow is where we put things we don't like about ourselves. This doesn't always mean they are bad things or traits that we need to change; for whatever reason, we have chosen to deny their existence. Don't be fooled, though; they still exist and are part of our daily lives however unconscious we are of their influence. My ego may refuse to acknowledge them, but they get projected onto other people. A simple example would be when I see someone on the road changing lanes without a blinker and think to myself in a very annoyed fashion how inconsiderate they are. Further down the road I unthinkingly do a similar thing, hitting my blinker at the very last second before making a turn. I justify my action as making sense but deny it makes equal sense for the driver who annoyed me earlier with the similar action. The reason they annoyed me is that, deep down, I know I'm often at fault for my own poor blinker habits. Rather than change *my* behavior, I project that guilt onto another who is doing the same thing, which makes me feel a bit better because it releases the emotion I feel toward myself. Long term, though, I will end up feeling worse because I'm pushing that attitude deeper into the shadow instead of fixing it. By putting it on someone else, I absolve myself of truly dealing with it. I get the easier less painful path of placing blame externally rather than fighting my ego and pointing the finger inward to resolve the issue.

When I admit my failure to use a blinker properly, I gain understanding and compassion for why someone would do the same and I no longer get mad at them. I may feel inconvenienced, but I do not have the offense feeling, as if they did it to me. That feeling of angry offense comes from the interplay between my shadow, ego, and subconscious. The shadow sees it as an attack for something it contains, then it causes the ego and subconscious to direct attention, anger, and offense outward instead of looking inward where painful things like realization of self as imperfect, acceptance of own issues, and inner development become obviously necessary. We do not see the world as it really is or people for who they are, we instead have a tendency to see the world through the lens of who we are, especially when it comes to the aspects of ourselves we hide, we project what we see as hidden failures onto others so they have to fix them instead of us having to fix them internally. When someone makes you mad always consider first how you are the problem.

Here's the short version of all that: Much of what you see in others good or bad is colored by your true self's view of you.

I like to imagine the psychological shadow as an actual shadow. The light shines on us from one side and the shadow comes off the other side, always avoiding the light. Light from one side projects the shadow onto and over other things or people. The darkness you see cast upon others is coming from you blocking the light.

The more transparent you become through honest internal reflection, the lighter the shadow you cast. Think of how a single light source casts a dark, well-defined shadow compared to several light sources. The more light sources there are, the fewer and smaller the shadows that are cast. Each point of view you add is another point of light that brightens your world and that of others.

When you cast a dark shadow onto another person, they become harder to see and even scary, like a monster in a closet. As you reduce the shadow you cast, you can see the other person's light more clearly, as they truly are. When more people shine their own light, your world becomes a brighter and happier place. There are fewer monsters hiding in those shadows.

Again, it starts with you taking the first step. A change in someone else won't stop your own shadow from being cast. The change needs to come from you. Ask yourself *why* someone annoys you or *why* you think they are bad. As you do, consider that there might be some way you think or some habit you have that you don't like about yourself or are trying to suppress. It's okay to find something, and in fact it's helpful when you do because you can better control that which you recognize in yourself, not what is in others. Maybe it's anger or envy or shame. Seeing *your* issues gives you more power over them while helping you to feel less persecuted by the good people around you who you thought were monsters. And the harder it is to find the thing in you that makes you think poorly of someone else, the more profound the change when you do uncover it.

And once you begin to unmask the dark shadow, your golden shadow becomes more visible. Remember that the golden shadow hides the good inside us and, like the dark shadow, gets projected as wondering, for example, "What makes them so special" or "I could never do that." By learning to see your golden shadow, you start to own your own goodness. And when you see an admirable act by another, it is easier to feel the joy and beauty of it instead of envy for something you think you lack – because you don't!

Shadow Language

Body language and facial expressions are the language of both our shadow and our true selves. The way these hidden aspects of ourselves can communicate from behind the mask of our ego. You can see other people's shadows through body language just as you can feel your own shadow trying to get your attention as your face and body react to what you or others are saying or what is happening around you.

Discovering the language of the body played a big role in learning about what lives inside others, but far more important is what it revealed about what was inside me. Seeing how other people express their innermost thoughts through movements, poses, and expressions is quite enlightening and sometimes a bit unsettling. Our faces and bodies are not very good at hiding the thoughts and emotions behind our words since our attention is either on what we are saying or how we look while saying it – not both. The reason watching others is a first step to understanding ourselves is because we don't often look within until we've seen something "out there" first.

Body language doesn't reveal that someone is a liar; it shows their personal levels of comfort with what they are saying. Multiple signs of discomfort can indicate intentional deception, but it can also show when people simply aren't in harmony with what they are expressing. Meaning their higher self knows a different truth than what they are speaking from habit or ego. Signs of harmony will look and feel much more aligned and comfortable. Initially, you won't be as skilled or willing to see your own body language as you are that of others. Our ego will often resist seeing something that might force us to make a change and/or tell a story about ourselves that is different from what we have identified with. The ego sees any change positive or negative as a type of death. It is trying to protect us from the pain of guilt, shame, and embarrassment that come with realizing we were wrong or not our best selves. This limits growth until we learn to love that feeling and recognize it as a tool rather than a pain.

We learn body language through observation of others and from the alignment practice I teach at the start of the book. The alignment practice tells us what a thought or feeling does to our own body or face and this allows us to read others better. However, we still have our ego in the way, so learning to observe these signs in others allows us to better see the ones we hide from ourselves. This creates another feedback loop where now we have more info and openness when doing the alignment practice, so we are learning more about ourselves that we can use to see more in others, and so the cycle continues.

So as a first step, observe when people are displaying signs and signals of harmony or misalignment. You can do this wherever people are expressing themselves; the world is your training ground. I suggest watching readily available online video content that you can rewind and watch again until you spot the signs. You can even try watching without sound since words can be a distraction. During these "exercises," try to be aware of your own biases – your own projections! If you start to feel a disconnect between what you tell yourself is correct and what your heart is saying, that's a sign of your own misalignment. Misalignment usually comes in the form of their facial expression not matching the words they are saying. Maybe they are shaking their head to indicate a negative when they are trying to convince you of something they know at some level isn't true. Perhaps they will shift in a way that moves 'away' or 'back' as a way of distancing themselves from something they or someone else said they dislike or want to hide from. Perhaps they will make a motion that blocks their eyes from the person they are speaking with in order to 'hide' from them, this is common when being deceptive either intentionally or subconsciously. A motion of hugging, holding, or petting oneself can be a way of calming related to an event they find upsetting.

As you watch the video content, look for signs of disharmony – not just intentional dishonesty but when someone is being unintentionally deceptive to further an agenda rather than furthering the truth. A worthy and honest point of view comes off very differently. It doesn't need deceptive or manipulative wording, nor will it need to make up or exclude points and facts.

Even if you agree with someone, try to identify where they stopped short of making a clear point and why they didn't ask a probing question. Did a question come to *your* mind that wasn't asked? Pause the video and look up that issue before they move to another point. As you get in this habit, you will start to catch people both in and out of your group being misleading in this way. Were their numbers a little suspicious? Did you accept them because you wanted to or because they were weak? Thinking of yourself, have you used language in a way that hides something that would invalidate your side of an argument? I have caught myself doing this many times and it feels like I am being scolded by my inner parent.

Of course, some people know they are being deceptive and will show different body language, for example, a "gotcha" smile or the smug smile of someone who is getting away with something, often called "duper's delight." Knowing they are pushing an agenda or lying to win an argument, they are getting exactly what they want from the lie and the quick smile shows it.

You can usually see and feel when someone is playing out a script. They get this very robotic look as if they are temporarily possessed – the person leaves while the script runs. Think of driving to work in a daze, unable to tell anyone how you got there. One of the "tells" is when someone uses colloquial expressions... "He looks rode hard and put up wet", "You can't eat your cake and have it too", or sayings such as these common to your region or group. If you catch yourself doing it, notice how you feel about that script. Did what you just said really resonate with what you truly believe, or was it just a programmed set of words you repeated without thought? Did you feel present when you said it, or did the script just run on its own for a second?

I often observe the individuals in political parties working against their true selves, because they've identified with the "party line" more than with their own hearts. I feel a great sadness to witness this whether I agree with their opinions or not. They are still people and I can see the pain they are causing themselves. This is a great example of something you would learn to see in another person before your ego would allow you to see it in your own expressions and actions. Once you recognize it you can see the pain and almost horror on their face as they seem forced to say something. Then when you find yourself getting that same feeling it is quite a wakeup call to examine your own beliefs and how they align with your heart. A good indicator is if you can welcome and clearly answer questions about your beliefs. If you get mad at questions then you have some soul searching to do, because someone who is aligned and truly believes in the side they are taking will welcome questions and the opportunity to have those beliefs challenged.

A person who speaks from their heart and soul radiates an energy of harmony and ease. Get someone talking about an activity or thing they love so much their inner nerd comes out, and it's like conversing with a happy child. This is the smooth road. You can see how the words flow out and it lights them up. You will often see their mask drop and their true self emerge in their facial expressions. You will feel this same soft comfort within yourself and in your face/body when you honestly share thoughts and feelings that you know are true for you. How amazing does it feel to be in that flow? When we give each other the space and safety to get in touch with such feelings, the essential goodness in people comes out.

When something doesn't align, however, we see the terror within others and ourselves. That disconnect between what is said and what is actually felt can trigger anger, rage, fear, sadness, contempt, and other potent emotions, even as the face futilely attempts to hide them. There is no longer a natural flow from that person's true beliefs. Those thoughts are being suppressed and masked by forced or deceptive words. Learning to pay attention to when the inner and the outer don't line up is an important step to discovering our shadows.

Be the Mirror

The practice of mimicking poses and facial expressions to see how they feel is very instructive. You will quickly notice that making a sad face makes you feel sadness. Making a surprised face fills you with a desire to look for what just surprised you. Taking a powerful pose like you just scored the winning goal can make you feel as if you could wrestle a lion, while the pose of fear with hunched shoulders and arms covering your face makes you feel like someone's next meal. Such practice will train you to start connecting poses with a particular feeling which will be of great value in understanding what you are overlooking or hiding from your general awareness.

The exercise I taught at the start of the book of relaxing your face and feeling the muscles as they tense and loosen will be of special benefit here. I invite you to try it (again) now. Mimic a face you saw someone make earlier in the day and acknowledge the emotions it brings up. Do you sense an inner and outer alignment or disharmony? If disharmony, does it feel strange to you, like it was you who said or did something wrong even though all you've done is mimic a pose? You can also flip it around and think of something with an emotion associated with it (positive or negative) and notice what muscles tense in your face. What expression are they trying to make?

Because we often deny certain feelings we don't want to admit exist, it's easier to see them expressed in others. When we do, our ability to see it in ourselves opens up. An example of this happens in groups. Let's say you come to believe something because that is what the rest of the group expects you to believe, even though it's actually not true for you (but you're not aware of that!). You have become a hostage of that group belief. You don't notice the lack of alignment or your facial expression until you see the expression in others. Now you know what to mimic, and it reveals new information to you about yourself.

As you start watching your own emotions, you will more easily see and understand them in others. When you see something expressed in another's face or movements, you will tie it both to how *you* felt mimicking that face/pose and to what was being discussed. You may look down and see your feet pointed toward the door when the annoying co-worker has cornered you for a boring conversation. Maybe your shoulders hunch and your head drops into the pose of a victim when your mean boss walks by. You will learn to control your body language to some degree, but for now I suggest just observing what you and others are doing and learning from it. Ask yourself, "Why did I do that?" "Why do I feel this way after that interaction?" "What is my posture when I'm around that person?"

When talking to people you consider friends, for example, do you find that you lean toward or away from them? This is your true self communicating that they are either good for you or not aligned with your best interest.

Does your face tighten around certain people? Perhaps your heart feels stress in their presence. Do you put body parts or objects between you and another? It may be that you are putting up a wall because you dislike or distrust them. Do you notice yourself mirroring someone by sitting the same way? This could indicate that your inner being likes and agrees with them.

There is great benefit in gaining a great understanding of body language through traditional learning methods and many great resources are available in the form of books and videos. At a primal level, though, we are naturally aware of most body language cues; we just don't pay attention to them. You know what a genuine smile looks and feels like; you can see and feel anger or contempt. As you practice and pay attention to such clues, your vocabulary for the shadow and the languages of the heart will increase.

Once you learn to understand the feeling of ideas that come from your true self – what you truly believe – and not what others think you should believe, you will start to realize that other people have true selves and that those feelings and thoughts are just as important and just as valid and should be respected as such. You don't necessarily have to agree with them – it's not about one person being right and the other one wrong. It's about people connecting to each other from their true selves without bias or prejudice.

When I used to lie to myself about who I was, pretending to be someone else to fit into a group I thought I needed or convincing myself that I believed in things I didn't, I had a very poor view of the rest of the world. I would project my deceptions on to other people and assume that if I was lying all the time – if I felt that dishonest feeling within myself – that must be how other people felt and went through their daily lives. The worst part is that I didn't intend to lie or even think I was lying. Once I started being honest with myself, I started having more compassion for others and seeing them as honest and upstanding and worthwhile.

Rough roads will mess up the alignment on your car which will then end up in the shop for costly repairs. The same is true with people. Those disharmonious thoughts and the lies we tell ourselves cause havoc on our minds and our bodies, resulting in damage that will be far more expensive to repair if not caught in time. Deal with small issues before they become big, and address those larger issues before they cause a catastrophic failure.

"I Have To"

How would you like to go around saying, "I do what I want, when I want, and how I want" and absolutely mean it?

No one likes it when someone walks up to you and says, "You have to ___." In fact, it often triggers a fight response. So why do it to yourself? Better yet, why do it to yourself many times each day?

Throughout my life, I have both said and heard others say things such as, "I have to walk the dog." "I have to take my children to the park." "I have to clean my house." These are not honest statements. You do not "have to" do any of them, you choose to.

Perhaps a better and more honest way to say it would be, "I enjoy walking my dog." "I want to clean my house so it's more comfortable." "I'm going to take the kids to the park."

Using the words "have to" implies that it's something you are being forced to do, which removes power and free will from yourself. To your subconscious mind, you are saying you do not control your life and should therefore look to other people and events to make decisions for you. You are saying that you are just a leaf being carried by the stream.

Watch how many times a day you lie to yourself and say; "I have to" do something. I still say it sometimes because that conditioning is deep. When I do catch myself saying it, I don't punish myself. I just observe and move on or go back and correct my statement to something more honest or direct: "I want to," "I get to," or at least, "I'm going to." Like with so many things, identifying and stopping such a feeling or statement communicates to your subconscious mind that this is not a thought you prefer or find beneficial. So learn to catch yourself when you say, "have to...," and correct it right there. You can also write "I want to" on your bathroom mirror or on a sticky note on your desk at work. It seems like a small thing, but establishing this habit is vital to gaining more control of your life. Over time it will have a huge impact.

Whether we are aware of it or not, we are all doing exactly what we choose and want to be doing, so it's technically accurate to say "I want to" instead of "I have to" because in reality you have already chosen to do it. This is important. You are making the choice to do the things you normally imply you are being forced to do, which is saying that you want to do one thing more than another, for whatever reason. Even if a gun were being held to your head, you are deciding to do that thing over the alternative.

A friend recently told me he had some anxiety about going to work the next day because he would "have to" deal with these particular people he let cause him the anxiety. I countered by saying that he did have a choice when he woke up in the morning to not get ready and to not go to work. It's a choice to get up, take a shower, drive to work, and spend the day there. I also said that he didn't have to wear a suit to work but he did because the benefits of having that job were stronger than his dislike for wearing the suit. Owning the choice puts you in control. When you realize you don't "have to," you are free and empowered. Now when you put on that suit, it's something you choose; it's not a burden.

When you say, "I want to" go to work because "I want to" pay my bills because "I want to" take care of my family, you are making a positive decision to take the action rather than suffer the consequences of resenting it or not doing it at all. The alternative – "I have to" go to work because "I have to" pay my bills because "I have to" take care of my family – implies you have no choice in the matter. But you always do.

Again, replace "I have to," "I need to," "I can't," "I must," or anything that implies you are compelled to do something with "I prefer to," "I choose to," "I want to," "I don't want to," or whatever affirms that you are in control. You can also add "I should" and "I shouldn't" to the list of what to avoid if they compel you to do something, but it's sometimes okay to use them when making certain choices... [such as].

By putting yourself in control and owning your choices, you will quickly find that your conscious and subconscious mind will fuel a feedback loop of self-empowerment.

You are Doing Exactly What You Want to be Doing

Once you decide that what you're doing is exactly what you want to be doing, you can view going to work from a different perspective. You can view cleaning the house from a different perspective. If you binge a TV show instead of cleaning the house, you are choosing to do that because it's what you honestly want to be doing at that moment. Watching the show and not cleaning your house may give you some short-term pleasure, but you will still need to decide if a dirty house honestly makes you less happy than watching the show makes you happy. Neither of these choices are good or bad, correct or incorrect, except as viewed through your feelings and choices for overall happiness.

For example, if you don't want to go to work, you will feel compelled to do it when you do. You could choose to move your family into a tent in the woods and perhaps you would be perfectly content there, but you are choosing to work to earn the paycheck to live in a nice home. You are more honest if you say to yourself in the morning that you want to go to work and that you are grateful for all the things that going to work provides. If you eat poorly or never exercise, you are making those choices for your own reasons. Once you embrace the idea you are choosing the things you "have to" do because you "want to" do them (assuming of course that you do!), they no longer feel like chores. They start to feel like blessings and part of your happiness in life.

As I mentioned earlier, when someone invites us to do something we prefer not to, we are trained to say, "I can't because I have to do this other thing." You just told them you aren't free to act with your own agency while normalizing a similar pattern for them. In short, you have contributed to your own enslavement as well as theirs.

It may seem like a tiny thing, but in reality you are telling a lie because what you really mean is that, for whatever reason, you would prefer to do something else instead of what the person is inviting you to do. We spend lots of time trying not to offend people with this type of response, but we don't usually consider that we ourselves do not like being lied to. If I consider lying to be a poor means of communication, it is reasonable to assume that other people feel the same way. Since each lie we tell makes an impact (however small) on our soul and our sense of well-being, it is best to avoid lying and encourage honesty in others through our own honesty.

The ultimate goal here is happiness – happiness for yourself and for those you interact with. If someone tells me they would prefer to do something other than what I've invited them to do, we'll have more of an opportunity for an open and honest dialogue about it. Perhaps my company isn't to their liking. This would be good for me to know because maybe I'm doing something I could change that would make myself more inviting to other people. Do I talk too much or stare at people in a way that is unsettling? Maybe they don't like the event I've chosen. Getting honest feedback on the event and why someone would prefer another activity can be useful for me in understanding what the people I like prefer to do. By learning about their preferences, we can have a pleasant conversation about the things they like without jealousy or judgment.

Another important possibility is that the person I'm interacting with feels an obligation to do an activity that isn't their preference but would rather do what I've invited them to. Maybe it's a family engagement or a work function and they're worried about what will happen if they don't attend. Now I know it's not about me or the event I've proposed.

If a situation comes up where you need to break a plan – especially if it has to do with something like focusing on your health – it doesn't hurt to tell others exactly that. By being honest, you may find that they become even more understanding. Instead of thinking of you as a flake, they will see you as someone who is honest and knows when to take care of themselves. Maybe they will feel freer to show you the same respect and honesty in the future. Maybe you create a place for more open personal dialog about yourselves where you both feel more connected and less like you have to deal with your issues on an island of you.

Allowing for honesty gives those around you permission to claim their own personal agency and makes it easier to increase your own level of personal agency and honesty while also normalizing personal agency for everyone.

Sweet Little Lies

Each lie erodes your soul. You can feel it, even the little lies. There is almost never a need to lie.

We know that lying is wrong and see liars as having lower value and being less likable. Can we then expect to see ourselves as having high morals and value if we lie? When we lie, we tell ourselves and our subconscious that we are incapable of upholding the moral that prohibits lying, essentially admitting that "I'm a liar." And it's a slippery slope. If you are already a liar, the next one won't really matter since you are already a person of lower moral character, and it also won't matter if you break this other moral as well. Once you're convinced that you are incapable of upholding morals, you disempower yourself from living a good and honest life.

When you say it's okay to lie, your brain will apply that to all situations; if it's okay to lie to people, well, I'm a person, so it must be okay to be lied to by others and even to lie to myself. Our closest feedback systems live inside us and affect us most directly. We decide what to feed those systems and can choose it to be positive or negative.

I often see people telling "white lies" so they do not hurt someone or to get out of a situation more easily. Adding the word 'white' in front of a lie doesn't change the fact you lied. Your subconscious gets another reinforcement that you are a liar, it does not distinguish between large and small, it only knows that you lied and that you easily violated your morals. This violation, as small as it may be, will take a little toll on your soul. Is it worth it? You can, with some practice, learn to find ways of not lying in these situations. For example:

Replace "I'm doing great" with "I'm a little frustrated today."

Why? There is no reason to hide how you feel, and perhaps they are frustrated as well, which could lead to a connection and both parties possibly resolving or releasing their frustration.

Replace "I can't go to your party because I have to___" with "I have something else I would prefer to do" or "I'm going to ___ instead."

Why? The dialog that follows this can go in many directions. Maybe their parties aren't fun because their dog is annoying but nobody tells them out of politeness. Now you started a conversation that may help them improve the experience for their guests. And the truth is you can go to the party if that is your preference.

Replace "You look great" with "I don't think that outfit is flattering on you."

Why? I care about my friends and want them to get the honesty they deserve from me. If they ask me how they look, and I lie, I do them no favors. The lie prevents real feedback that could tell them an outfit or personal care issue prevents people from seeing them at their best. If I (diplomatically) tell my buddy that he dresses like a bum and could be in better shape, that could start him on a path where he gains more confidence and meets the girl of his dreams.

I have found that honest answers can create dialog that leads to closer connections with those you encounter and a better self-image at the end of the day. But we are used to the comfort of little lies, making true honesty seem harsh. Isn't it funny that we consider it polite to lie? Talk about being inconsistent. We tell our children that lying is bad, and then model them to lie several times a day by our actions. When we lie, it's as if we are talking through a plastic mask, and then we get plastic masks in return. When I'm honest and take off my mask, I invite others to take off their masks as well. This means I get to see more real people and thus more of their beauty which makes my day and world a much nicer place. You are making honesty and openness more normal for those around you as well as for yourself.

Think of how many movie plots would have been much less complicated had the characters just been honest and dealt with the initial issue rather than lying and letting it turn into a monster. But then, such is the source of drama and strife, which we can't seem to get enough of.

Friends Don't Let Friends Lie

If a friend is saying something deceptive or immoral, I find it beneficial to call them out. This can be done at whatever level of politeness you are comfortable with. Otherwise, ignoring that injustice and letting them slide allows the energy of that deception to later be relayed to another person and then another where it may spread (however subtly) and the world becomes a slightly less awesome place. It is far better to catch a friend deceiving themselves because you'll be normalizing honesty within your group and making it okay for people to call out others when they see it. And when *you* get called out for something, you can decide if you want to make a change that will help your alignment and happiness.

When someone we like says something we know is wrong, it creates a disharmony in us. We can feel the machinery of our mind working to justify and accept it because they are in our group. But if we say nothing about it, we allow the lie to keep propagating, both inside and outside of us. When someone says something we know in our heart is true, there is no need to justify anything; it feels right and smooth. But be careful that you don't confuse a habitual agreement with something that aligns with your inner being. Pay attention to the clues and you'll be able to distinguish between what feels safe to your ego from what

feels authentic to your heart.

Morals

"I could not say I believe. I know! I have had the experience of being gripped by something that is stronger than myself, something that people call God."
—Carl Jung

Feeling part of something bigger helps to reduce fear because you are not just an isolated island in the sea but rather a part of that sea. It is a place you can always return to when you need to feel safe, protected, and stable.

Something Bigger

Your morals should be definite, consistent, and bigger than you, your environment, your group, your religion, or your circumstances. Your morals are your "god." When you follow them, you feel blessed and rewarded but when you violate them, you feel as if you are being punished. I'm not suggesting that you deny or replace a religious god. Whether or not that god exists, you will always have your morals and true self to answer to.

We can develop or inherit a base set of morals from a religion or group, but ultimately it is up for each of us to decide what our specific personal morals are. They may be the same or similar as that religion or group, but we can decide what they are for ourselves. Your personal wellbeing will come from finding and sticking to your own established and clearly defined sense of right and wrong. That all said, starting with a foundation of morals from a religion or group is often a good place to begin.

I am not religious in a traditional sense and would be inclined to call myself an "agnostic theist," which means I believe there is something bigger than me, but I can't define it. I can appreciate the religious and the non-religious as I have been both at different times in my life. I say this because I want to be clear that I respect both positions even though some research shows that those who tend toward religion and spirituality are generally happier than those who are less religious.

The reasons are debatable, but I think the more spiritually or religious inclined have a sense of being part of something bigger than themselves; they have a sense of purpose in serving a "higher being." If you aren't presently religious, you likely won't be able to simply turn on a belief in a higher power. So I invite you to do something equally as valuable by making the higher power your own morals. They will make great judges of your actions. For the currently religious, I invite you to compare the morals of your religion to those that resonate most deeply in your inner being.

For example, those who believe in evolution accept that we have base instincts that control our behaviors in order to help us reproduce and continue our species – which lowers the role of free will. Accepting this makes it honorable when you can overcome those built-in controls. On the other hand, creationists can say they were created with a blank slate and granted complete free will by a creator. The beauty of this is the power and responsibility that come with having free will and then choosing to use it honorably. Either way, displaying more control over our instincts or directing our free will in a positive way leads to more happiness once you see them for what they are.

Another benefit of being religious or spiritual is the role of introspection and how such people are more inclined to question whether they are living up to their firm moral principles and expectations. But whether or not you're religious, contemplation of what is important to your higher self is a powerful practice.

Feeling part of something bigger helps to reduce fear because you aren't just an isolated island in the sea but rather a part of that sea. It's a place you can always return to when you need to feel safe, protected, and stable. You can think of definite, clear, consistent, and (usually) simple morals as something bigger to feel a part of. They represent a kind of authority to which you can ask; "Am I handling this situation to the best of my ability and in a way I can gain self-respect and pride from?" There is a feeling of security in knowing that you always have a wise inner advisor you can turn to. Think of your morals as a representation of "god".

Too often we want to remove or deny something called "God" from our lives because we associate it with a bad experience or perhaps a loss of freedom. But instead of just denying the religious God, we also end up denying and ignoring the *internal* god represented by our morals. We begin to conflate the two, seeing our internal morals as bad and oppressive as well. Your internal morals are with you all the time, and whether or not there is a religious God doesn't matter to those morals. They will judge you, punish you, and reward you as they consider appropriate no matter how much you try to deny or ignore what they say.

Don't entirely dismiss a group or religion when selecting morals because we want to stay open to learning from others who may have valuable opinions based on something we aren't fully aware of. To say that religious people are dumb or atheists are evil limits what you can learn from "those people". I thought religious people were crazy when I was an atheist and that atheists needed moral help when I was religious. It turns out that both were capable of great morals in their own way and I'm glad I was able to see it from both sides.

Assuming that you are who you will always be and that your values will never change are guaranteed to keep you from growing as a human being. Stay open to whoever and whatever your future self says is right, not what is easy in the moment.

Once you've landed on a solid set of morals that fit who you currently are and want to be as a person, stick with them. If you don't, you devalue them and the efforts it took to make them yours. You also devalue yourself by telling your mind that you aren't capable of following a set of values. An example would be a moral of non-aggression. To honor that moral, I would never initiate violence toward another, or steal from them, or violate their freedoms and right to life. If I did, I would be violating myself and my morals.

Shifting, inconsistently applied, and flexible morals will always leave us feeling dissatisfied. We do not get the pride of sticking to them because we know they could have changed at any time to meet our current desire. We also do not get the shame and guilt necessary for personal growth when we do not stick to those flexible morals, because we simply shift them to make them fit what we did or are doing, this allows us to falsely claim that we did follow our morals, but our subconscious knows the truth.

The golden rule applies when determining your morals. I don't like being lied to, so lying violates my morals. I don't like having my things stolen, so I shouldn't steal things from others. I have a fondness for being alive, and assume that others feel the same and shouldn't be murdered. If violence is bad, then it should be bad against my friends *and* my enemies. Seems pretty obvious, but it can be harder to apply than we want to admit due to our loyalties to those in our groups compared to those outside our groups.

Changing your mind about right and wrong based on who is committing the act will also create a dissonance within your mind. The offense you feel when your friend is rude to a waiter should be the same as when you see a random person doing the same. If your friend picked on or insulted someone, is that more acceptable than if someone picked on your friend?

I have found that a moral is aligned with my inner being if I can honestly say I would not want it done to or by my child or loved one. We can lower the bar for ourselves, but we wouldn't do so when it comes to those we love, especially a child. So If I'm okay with something being done to or by my child or loved one, it has passed the test.

Inconsistent Morals Are Not Morals, They Are Tactics

There will be times when circumstances make it hard to stick to a particular moral. When that happens, we shouldn't alter the moral; we should admit we are violating it. This keeps us from shifting and adapting morals to fit our current needs and situations, rather than trying to change or prevent the situation, so we can better conform to our morals. Be open to setting new definitions for your morals as you go through life, but be sure that you make those changes from your heart and not based on convenience. The moral itself should remain and every effort should still be made to avoid violating it.

Let's say I have a moral that says stealing is wrong. It must apply to all stealing. If I say it is not okay to steal but it's okay to steal from rich people, I am not being consistent or honest with myself and I will cause a disharmonious feeling. How can I ever feel fully good about not violating a moral if it's only applied when convenient? Consider this: The harder it is to stick to a moral, the better it feels when you do – especially when it involves someone you don't like.

There will be times in life when violating a moral is an unfortunate but seemingly necessary option. Let's say your family is starving and you think you must steal food to feed them. If you have flexible morals, you won't try other methods of obtaining food first; you will likely jump right to stealing. You may tell yourself it was done for a greater good, but you still violated a moral and must recognize that each time you do, you begin to shift that behavior in your mind toward becoming an acceptable behavior. In other words, one can get used to violating a moral so it's easier the next time.

We are very adaptable creatures who will make mental and physical changes based on our environment. The problem is that to violate a moral only seems easier on the surface. In your heart you will know, and there will be disharmony between your effort to rationalize it and the feelings you have about what you did. That "god" within is always watching; it will not hesitate to "punish" you, even for the misdeeds that you have come to consider normal. We all know what that feels and should be grateful it happens to help us stay on the right track.

To say, then, that stealing is wrong unless I'm stealing from someone who has more than I do is not a definite or consistent moral. Where do we draw the line? Can I steal from someone who has a dollar more than me? Can I steal the more expensive product because I can only afford the store brand? No. The moral says that stealing is bad, and I dishonor and devalue myself and the god within by trying to make it okay for any reason.

We can likely agree that hurting or killing another person is bad for many reasons. We can also agree that in the most extreme circumstances, it can be necessary. If you have to hurt a violent aggressor to save yourself or another person, you have undoubtedly done the right thing, but you must also acknowledge that you did so in violation of your moral that says killing or hurting is wrong. If you consider violence and killing as wrong, you will work to find alternatives to either before resorting to such measures. Perhaps you will try to scare an attacker away or give them a warning. Maybe you will try to use logic and reason before resorting to violent options.

Even taking pleasure in or celebrating an injury to someone because they are on a different team or have an ideology different than yours violates the "no violence" moral. There is honor in feeling compassion for the pain of those on the other side. When you do, you are showing respect for others while telling yourself that you, too, are deserving of compassion and respect.

The taking of a life is bad no matter the reason. Even if it seemed the only option, it was still a violation of your moral imperative that says killing is bad, and an extreme example of admitting you exhausted all other options before making that choice. Yes, if someone broke into my house to hurt me or another, or if I saw someone getting attacked on the street, I would do whatever it took to stop that violence, but I wouldn't accept the violence I used as normal or within my morals. That line must never be moved; stepped over however briefly and necessarily, but never moved. We need to clearly understand when we are within our morals and when we have gone outside of them.

Group Morals

Putting the power of deliberate intention into your morals prevents you from being pulled along by the intentions of a group or another person. When you lack intention, the influence of the others who do have intention becomes, by default, more powerful than yours. The stronger intention will win, so by honoring yours and upholding your morals, you will keep from being swept away with the rest of the crowd.

Weighing your morals against those of your group, religion, friends, job, or political party should be done regularly to verify that you aren't just going along with theirs, especially if those morals have shifted over time into something that no longer match yours. It is not uncommon to find yourself wondering how you came to agreeing with things that don't align with your internal compass. The most likely reason is that you stopped paying attention and/or it was easier to just go along with the group. Some flexibility is great to allow growth, but if you build yourself on sands that shift too often, your morals will change along with that sand. You thought you were building in one direction only to notice that your front door is in your backyard!

There are many instances in history that can serve as warnings to be careful. Remember that a politician has one job, and it is not to make the world a better place. It is to get re-elected. Sure, they may start their career with noble intentions. But once their income and security are tied to getting votes, their morals will shift to what gets them more votes rather than to what is right or what they truly believe. If you've identified with a politician or a party rather than your morals, you can easily be carried along as their actions and principles follow the political winds.

A political party can become a religion without moral controls or self-reflection. Don't let that happen to you.

Pay attention to when your political party is encouraging your fear or asking you to repeat chants and slogans, these are ways we willingly trick ourselves into giving up control and power to the group instead of considering our thoughts and actions carefully. When you want to stir up a mob, feed them energy that makes them afraid of or angry at "the enemy." The chants that start during protests and riots, for example, have a rhythm that hijacks our brains. When I hear such chants, I know it's time to leave to prevent my mind from being controlled and because I don't have any trust in the good intentions and actions of those already under that control. They are no longer using their own sense of morals and values; they have given themselves over to a crowd of unknown intent.

A job can often cause us to betray our values because our livelihood depends on keeping those paychecks coming. Upton Sinclair said: "It is difficult to get a man to understand something when his salary depends upon his not understanding it." The source of that paycheck has a power over us, sometimes causing us to give a little on what we consider right. Your job may ask you to take advantage of another employee or a customer to make money. You may not agree but you remember that paycheck so it's easier to justify. You may be asked to lie on some numbers or hide some illegal activity and you may do it because you want to feed your family. Again, do what you *need* to do but know it will affect your opinion of yourself. You can't pee upstream, which is a way of saying that what you put into a system will affect both you and others. If your morals are solid, then no matter what your boss or someone else in any organization does to influence those morals, you can intentionally decide to put only good action into the stream.

Perhaps the group of friends you've known since college have turned to drinking or shady business and personal dealings. Maybe you get pulled along as the goal posts of what is acceptable change. Maybe your group has always been into partying but that no longer fits into your morals. Acceptable behavior can also vary by culture and family environment. Either way, if something was once considered acceptable but now you decide it's wrong, make a change and live the life and morals that are right for you. You can always invite those friends to come with you on a different journey, but always give yourself permission to leave incompatible groups in order to do what is right for your wellbeing. Who knows? There may be others in that group who also want to change and you can be their catalyst. Or the new groups your improved self meets may propel you even higher.

HIHO

When you stray from what is right *for you*, you reduce your capacity to feel good about who you are which reduces your capacity for overall happiness. Who feels better: The person who sticks to their morals no matter the circumstance or the one who changes their morals to make a passing situation more convenient? You are your morals, and they will stay in place as long as they serve the current version of you. Also, if you tend to be afraid or angry, you are more vulnerable to the morals of others. Sticking to your morals will help reduce those feelings because your morals, purpose, and intent are bigger than any emotion you feel.

When I put out to the world that it's okay for me to follow my own moral path by speaking and acting in that manner, I make it more acceptable for others to do the same. I put into the system what I want to get back from it. When others follow their own higher path after seeing me do it, they are making it even easier for me to follow that path to internal happiness.

Guilt and Forgiveness

"I could tell you my adventures—beginning from this morning," said Alice a little timidly, "but it's no use going back to yesterday, because I was a different person then."
—Lewis Carroll, *Alice's Adventures in Wonderland*

Guilt, shame, compassion, and empathy are all part of a moral system designed to keep us on the right track so that we treat other beings well and can feel proud of ourselves when we behave according to our morals. Guilt and shame become tools for personal growth. When we learn to appreciate and not fear them, we have more power over how we handle them.

Rewards and Punishments

Guilt and shame are valuable internal punishments for not following what compassion and empathy tell us is right. They encourage us to change our negative patterns, keeping us feeling that we can do better. If I were to hit and injure someone, I would feel horrible for what I had done. If I were to commit a theft or assault and knew that no one would see or catch me, I would still be punished by thinking of myself as a less than honorable person. I would lose self-respect, and in order to not feel that pain, I would push these unwanted aspects into my shadow where they will project onto others I encounter. As discussed earlier, it's easier to call someone else terrible for something I don't like about myself than to own it and fix it.

When it comes to guilt and shame, we can get stuck in those cycles. Two ibuprofen will take care of a headache and help us to feel better, but taking the entire bottle will have quite opposite effects. It's the same with guilt and shame; a little is enough to help us grow. Taking on more than necessary can tear us apart with debilitating mental and physical side effects. Appreciate the guilt and shame for helping you stay on the right path, change your patterns to align with your true self, and then let them go.

How Did I Get Here?

Imagine a party where people are playing a board game. One of the players needs to leave, so they call you in to take their place. You sit at the table and instead of starting at the beginning, you play from where they are in the game. Your piece already has its place on the board, and you have inherited the resources and problems the previous player had.

You can see they didn't play the game to your standards and you are sure you can do better. Do you feel guilt or shame for the moves and choices they made? Of course not; you just jump in and make the best of the situation you started with.

Each day we are stepping into a game in progress, always starting with the game board laid out as it is. We can lament the past that got us to this point or disconnect from the previous players and move forward from where we are now. We are always starting from the present no matter what good or bad was done in the past. The future you will have the same perspective on the present you that present you has on your past self.

Now think of yourself as a board game. Your ego would look at it and say, "I am playing this, so the decisions that got me here must be me." Fortunately, your ego is wrong a lot. It assumes that nothing has changed, but it's up to your true self to decide if you've changed enough to call yourself a new person. Maybe you are only a new person in certain areas where you have managed to resolve patterns that weren't suited to your new best self and you still have other patterns that need work. In those resolved and changed areas, you *are* a new person. Accepting that change allows you to see that change is possible and that you are not tied to being the old you. Now you can change even further because you see and accept that it's possible to do so.

You are responsible for the past just as you are responsible for the moves made in the game before you joined it. Your debt from your past is still your debt. Perhaps you still have a family or pets you are taking care of. This is not about walking away from life but de-attaching from the old you and how he or she handled things. It's about the game you are playing now, with its own circumstances and rules. Your game piece is still on the board where the previous player left it. Now go do your best to win. The same will be true tomorrow.

You will likely and deservedly feel guilty if you haven't sufficiently changed as a person since an offense you caused yourself or others. If you have changed as person since that event, you are giving yourself keys to that mental prison. Whereas someone who is still the same as they were or has not resolved the pattern they were in will still remain in that mental prison. This is much like how society imprisons people until we can be sure that their offending pattern has been altered. Physical jails try to deliver the punishment that would otherwise have come from the guilt people *should* have felt to prevent themselves from committing crimes against others.

Other players in the game could try to insult you for how poorly you've been playing, but if you aren't the person who made those moves and decisions, the insults should have no power. Similarly, insulting your past self as if it were your present self binds you to that past self and can cause you to behave as that past self would, since in your mind, the two are the same. When you break that association, the self-loathing and shaming has as much effect on your psyche as if the insults were directed at someone else entirely.

Patterns

We must admit that change is not only possible but normal for ourselves and others. Once we do, we can stop identifying with our past selves and we can stop identifying others with their resolved pasts.

Repeating behavioral patterns from our past that keep causing the shame and guilt also happens and ties us to that past self. If you are still making those same poor choices, you are still your past self, but at least now you know where you can work to improve.

As we resolve those behavioral patterns that cause us to violate our morals, we can let go of the guilt for not having acted as we wish we had and separate ourselves from the former self that was stuck in those patterns. Resolving those patterns gives us the freedom to move forward.

When you carry guilt for negative patterns that you have already resolved it is like being mad at yourself today, because from the perspective of your future self you are handling the current situation poorly. Future you will have resolved present patterns and developed a presently unknown method for handling the present situation with more elegance. Your past self didn't know what you know now and so handled things to the best of its ability – no matter how poorly. Your present self does not know what your future self will know, so your present self is handling things to the best of its ability….

You've heard the phrase, "I would have handled that differently."

Since "I" would have done that differently, then it must have been a "they" who handled it poorly in the past. It wouldn't make sense to say, "I would handle what I am doing now differently." If you haven't learned from your mistakes and haven't grown as a person, then it is "I" (you!) who made that past mistake. If you have grown and changed patterns, then it is "they" who made that mistake, rather than "I".

I am handling it to the best of my ability now and they handled it to the best of their ability then. Do you feel guilt for pooping your pants as a baby? That was your capacity then, but you are not that child anymore. You have learned better control over that aspect of your life; you and your capacity have changed.

This also makes admitting to past mistakes much easier for the ego to handle because it's not talking about itself when it says an error was made; the ego is allowed to feel that it's talking about someone else who made that mistake.

Change your Picture

What if we could take a picture of the "average human" of each generation and put them all into a long file cabinet. The photos right next to one another would look essentially the same, while the images thousands of generations apart would show big differences. Now think if we did this with your life – take a picture each day and put into a file. From one day to the next, you would look pretty much the same. But images from 10 or 20 years ago would show significant differences. In some cases, you might see a huge change in a shorter period of time based on unexpected events.

Now imagine that photo as a snapshot of both physical features as well as personality. You get to decide by the choices you make how different you want the picture tomorrow to be from the one taken yesterday. Unfortunately, we spend much of our lives tied to our past, and the idea of making significant changes to who we are fundamentally is not something we often think about as possible. This keeps the image from last year looking much like the one from today.

We go through life more rigid than we probably like to admit. Data from your cell phone can be used to predict your future behavior with about 93% accuracy. We drive the same way to work, we go to either the same places or the same types of places at similar times and days. This applies to what we think, how we react, who we hang out with, and what we consume (food, content, and information).

You can choose to alter the patterns and habits that keep you from feeling proud of who you are now. Don't be afraid to intentionally become someone very different from your past; this, now, is your life. Learn something new; do something you know in a different way; make new friends; disconnect or reconnect with people as it serves you presently; form a new habit, drop and old habit. There is plenty you can do to detach yourself from the past.

And when we do, our minds become more flexible and open to and capable of changing patterns and routines. The process takes advantage of the brain's *neuroplasticity*, which literally means its ability to change its structure in response to both internal and external influences. And so we can absolutely make huge changes in our life and lose the guilt we may feel for something our less mature self may have done.

If I Can, You Can

There is a thought experiment that asks if you can prove that the universe was not created yesterday. In this the universe was created yesterday as if it had been going on for billions of years with all matter, actions, and memories confirming that timeline. You see, it cannot be proven false, in the same way you cannot prove anything exists outside of your consciousness. What would you do if that were true? Would you still go to work and stop by the grocery store? You would remember your life as if you had lived it, but did you? Should you feel any guilt or shame for it, or should you just move forward since that is the only direction you can go?

This means the universe was just created for others as well...

In order to show ourselves capable of detaching from our past, we must accept that others are also capable of doing

119

so. We are all the same and equal, right? To say that other people aren't capable of detaching from their past selves tells my mind that I, too, am incapable of changing who I am from who I was. To appreciate that people are not their past allows us to appreciate and allow our own ability to grow into someone new.

But You Said ...

People trying to find something hurtful or offensive in another person's life are unknowingly causing harm to themselves. They are taking something that no longer has effect or power and bringing it back to life to cause more harm. Someone digging into the past of a person who isn't displaying a pattern from that past is saying that they themselves are unable or unwilling to change and must therefore project that inability or unwillingness onto another person. We can either act to improve ourselves or try to hold others back from improving by tying them to their past. One way or another, our minds want to feel better about ourselves, in comparison to them, or simply for the sake of our own improvement.

There are several stories of famous people who spent their careers participating in and encouraging debauchery or worse. Then they shifted their thinking and changed their moral stance and now want to be accepted for their new ways. Should they be held accountable to their old behaviors or should we accept them for who they have become? They can both be accountable for their past and they can be accepted and honored for changing their life patterns. Are we jealous because they changed while we are still replaying their old albums or movies, wondering why we are stuck being who we have always been? Do we want to pull them down to where they were and we still are? Do we want to hold them back to make ourselves feel better for not growing? Or can we praise and encourage them for improving and thus show ourselves that we too can make amazing changes?

Forgiveness is not necessary

The question of forgiveness is about who is doing the forgiving and who is being forgiven. Forgiveness is closely tied to the system of internal punishment described when speaking of guilt. It only applies if those involved have not grown and if they have not grown it is helpful to their growth.

If the person who committed the offense has grown as a person and no longer has the patterns that caused them to commit the offense, then who is being forgiven? You would be forgiving someone that no longer exists. You can certainly forgive them and remind them of who they were in the past, just like you would love someone to bring up your past and reminding you of what a jerk you were. To unnecessarily tie someone to their past tells our mind that the past is who we will always be as well.

If they have not grown into a new person as far as those patterns are concerned your forgiveness does them a disservice by removing the fuel they have to resolve those patterns and grow as a person.

If I was wronged by someone and I have since grown as a person I am no longer the person that was wronged or allowed myself to be wronged, so who would be doing the forgiving? Would it be a version of myself that no longer exists? How would they pull that off from wherever non-existence is? If I have grown as a person and into a new person I am not the one who would need to forgive. If I feel I need to forgive then I should ask myself where I can grow further so I do not feel tied to that past self who was hurt.

I don't like the word "forgiveness." I prefer to think of it as understanding that a person was acting to the best of their ability and then allowing yourself to notice if their bad patterns have been resolved. To think of ourselves as detached from our past requires that we also see others as

122

having the ability to grow and become their better selves, so we need not forgive or be forgiven.

Capacity

You can only improve as far as your ability to recognize and understand what better is. Said differently, you are always as good as your current capacity allows. When I speak of current capacity, it doesn't mean you at your best moment on your best day. It means the best you can act in a situation as it is and how you are at that time. Some days my best capacity is laying on the couch, eating pizza, and playing video games. On other days I get a ton of work done and manage to be kind to many people. To increase this capacity means I need to do more of the things I am proud of more often. So, an increased capacity means I still eat the pizza on a day I am less proud of, but maybe I do laundry that day too. Then on another not so great day, I eat the pizza, do the laundry, and solve the hard problem of consciousness. Taking steps forward is what matters, not if they are big or small.

That increase in capacity is another thing that will separate us from our past selves. If you want to disconnect from guilt, find ways to increase your capacity and understanding.

Yes, we make mistakes, but those mistakes – as well as our successes – show what our capacity was at that time. Our capacity can be high or low in any given moment, such as having a great day and then you get annoyed at the talkative person in line in front of you. That was your capacity at that moment. Steps backwards can be useful in their ability to mirror what you may be doing or avoiding out of fear or habit. The fact that you can recognize moments when you've acted below your ultimate capacity is how you train yourself to strive for alignment with that higher capacity.

There are two things we can do to resolve the guilt we feel for present actions. First, we can make sure we are presently acting to the best of our capacity. If we thoughtfully decide we are honestly doing our best, we have nothing to feel guilty about since we are already doing as well as we can. Second, take steps to increase your capacity through intention and introspection. Give your future self the gift of capacity you can both be proud of.

Altruism

"He who was ready to sacrifice his life, as many a savage has been, rather than betray his comrades, would often leave no offspring to inherit his noble nature."
— Charles Darwin

The internal reward we get from doing kind deeds for others is what encourages us to continue wanting to do those kind deeds. Without this built-in payoff, we would lose the motivation to be kind. No matter how hard you try, you are not selfless or altruistic. In fact, the harder you try, the less you are.

You are not Altruistic (and that is Beautiful)

Much like a unicorn, altruism sounds really neat, but does not exist in us. If altruism were real for us, we would have no motivation to be kind. Altruism is selflessly doing for others without expecting or getting a reward. This is not possible in the presence of free will, and the word should only be used in the animal kingdom where instinct replaces free will. The level to which we as humans have free will is a huge question, but for the purposes of this conversation we will assume we have it in abundance.

You won't necessarily be a better person by being kind, but you certainly can help yourself and others feel better. For you, there is a sense of pride for having done a good deed; for the other person, there is the feeling of being a little less alone in the world. Both of you will carry that extra bit of happiness into the world.

When we strive to be altruistic, we are striving to not be rewarded for being kind. The brain gets confused when you try to feel bad for feeling good, because you are told by society you should get no reward for being kind, and yet you do feel good. You feel good and proud, either for doing the kind deed or for the pride for not feeling good for doing the kindness. Feeling proud of yourself for feeling guilty for feeling joy for doing good deeds, that is about the longest most convoluted way of feeling good for being kind I can imagine. One way or another you are going to feel good for being kind, so why not just take the shortest path?

This "feeling good" is a reward. Once we accept that it's okay to receive a reward for our kindness, we no longer feel disharmonious and can then seek that feeling freely, without guilt, by doing more kind acts.

126

The only way you can help someone and not get rewarded for it is by accident, when you never intend it or know about it. Maybe you kick a rock in a parking lot for fun which knocks a nail out of the path of a car that would have run over it. In this case, while there's a potential net positive, neither of you knew anything happened.

I used to think I was super awesome because of how often I would help other people and not expect anything in return. Helping others with projects they were struggling with; holding doors for people; even helping people I didn't really know to move their furniture from one house to another. Then it hit me...

I started to realize (admit) that everything I did had a built-in personal reward or value—even when the payment comes in the form of my ego enjoying the bliss of how great and kind I am. I am rewarded in status (honored by my group, impressing the ladies, or making new friends). I always got some kind of reward, and that's why I kept doing those things. I was, in the end, being quite self-serving. But there is nothing wrong with admitting that I do things for others because it provides me a benefit, especially if that benefit is a warm feeling in my heart. This is about happiness, so any way I allow myself to feel that true happiness more often the better.

This good feeling within is the only reward we are really entitled to and can reliably count on receiving. I cannot control or expect another person to reward me for what I consider a kind action. Sometimes I hold the door for someone without getting even a glance of acknowledgment. If I needed a reward from someone for my good acts, I would be setting myself up for disappointment because it may never happen and I would become less motivated to perform such acts if they only took place in secret.

Were I truly altruistic, it wouldn't annoy me to be ignored by the person I just held the door open for. When they ignore me, they deny me part of the reward I was seeking through my kindness. Yes, I still get to feel like a hero, but where is their approval and smile of appreciation? To react like this tells me I didn't do it for them. I did it for myself.

You go to work to provide a service and you get paid for that service. No matter how much you like your work, you don't do it for free. The salary you get pays bills. Similarly, when we do kind acts, we are paid in happiness and pride which fuel the soul. Even the ultimate sacrifice of giving one's life for another person or cause comes with a sense of honor and knowledge that your name will be remembered, or you'll have a last glorious moment of pride.

As a society, we would do a lot better by being honest with ourselves about our motivations because we would then see how our positive and negative actions affect the system and how the system then affects us. Anyone who says they are doing something for you or others without need for a reward is not being honest with themselves or possibly not being honest with you. Beware of people who are so involved in supporting your cause that they seem to neglect their own. They may be intentionally dishonest or subconsciously dishonest – it's hard to say which is more damaging or dangerous.

I have found that people who are too eager to help others or come to their defense aren't usually being honest with themselves about their intentions. They are more like drug addicts than moved by altruistic intent. The pleasure centers in our brains that come alive when doing a drug like cocaine are the same as when we do a good deed. Once addicted to this feeling, one can easily start to see the reward as more important than the act that led to the reward – the way an addict justifies stealing from another person to get that next hit. When we are too quick to come to the aid of another, we are taking some of their power away so we can get our little bump of pleasure chemicals. We will even infantilize others and make them feel like they cannot succeed on their own so that we can get our hit of that sweet crack pipe of altruism. If I tell someone they cannot make it in life because they are a certain race or sex, I am not helping them; I am helping myself feel like a hero at their expense. I am keeping them in victimhood so I can keep getting my dose of dopamine by acting as their hero. I have a reward based on their continued suffering and dependency.

Consider the old saying: "Give a man a fish and feed him for a day, teach a man to fish and feed him for a lifetime." You can keep getting your little hits of dopamine by giving fish away and keeping that man dependent on you, or you can get a long lasting supply of dopamine knowing that you helped someone improve their life and become empowered. I call this long lasting and stronger dose of dopamine "medical grade kindness".

Helping others too much also prevents them from growing. It maintains your position of superiority because if they never get to learn to be self-sufficient, they will always need to look to you or others for help. You get to feel good about helping but you forget the other side of that coin. It's like squirrels who learn to eat from feeders and lose the necessary skills to survive in the wild on their own. Helping too much can be more about your ego than simply giving others a helping hand.

I would do better for both of us to help them see where they are powerful. Not lying to them by saying they are perfect but helping them see they can do anything they want. They get support and I still get my hit of dopamine. Plus, I have put into my feedback loop the idea that people are powerful no matter who they are. Which means that I as a person, am also more empowered.

While the desire to give makes us feel like we are doing good in the world, we must temper that instinct, because receiving from others is also a noble act. It both affirms our value as a human being and gives others the chance to get their own dopamine hit. We often forget that trying to achieve our goals and dreams of helping people can be at the expense of the empowerment of those same people.

You can absolutely help other people be happy, but that shouldn't be your focus; your focus should be on making *yourself* happy, which by example gives others permission to find their own happiness. If I try to *make* someone else happy, it will likely frustrate both of us if the desired results aren't achieved.

I encourage everyone to be kind and to do their best to make the world a happier and better place. Just be honest with yourself about why you are doing it. The importance of honesty and intentions will be covered in more depth later in the book, but they influence nearly every aspect of our lives in a world where dishonesty and hidden motivations have become normal. Consider if you are truly helping someone or if you are just trying to make yourself look better to others and in your own eyes. I know I had a lot of thinking to do once I looked at my true motivations. I found many cases where I thought I was being kind but, from a broader view, could see that I was actually doing harm.

Finite Resources

You cannot know what is best for another, so the best you can ever do is to act honorably according to your true self. Helping yourself in a system designed to help everyone is your best chance to be useful.

The cells in my knee do not know of or care about the cells in my liver. They are not knowingly working toward the benefit of the liver, but they aren't working against it either. Destroying the system is not in their best interest. Each cell and body part is taking care of itself and by doing so is taking care of the whole body.

The same principle applies to a work environment, household, community, country, or any other group. When management reduces the pay of workers to get more money for stockholders, it runs the risk of only attracting and keeping less productive workers. When one spouse betrays another, they break a system that was to the benefit of their children and therefore to themselves and the entire society.

The ego used properly tells us how we fit into the machine of the world. It can show me that my actions to cooperate with you are actions also taken to my benefit. It will also show that actions I take against you will break down that elegant machinery.

An action is not kind or unkind; it is just an action that is interpreted by yourself or another. We each decide if an event is good or bad based on how it affects us and how we feel about it.

Imagine yourself in heavy traffic backed up to a light that has just turned green and cars are starting to move. You see someone trying to exit a parking lot and merge into traffic in front of you. You make the choice to be kind to that driver and let them in. Now you have given them a great feeling because they received kindness and you get the wave of good feelings that come with helping someone. But there are other moving parts; the system is bigger than you and the person you let in. There is a car behind you that may not make the light because you let in that car in front of you.

That driver doesn't think you did a good deed and are possibly annoyed to be waiting for yet another red light. Maybe they will now be late for an important event or the ice cream they just bought for the kids will further melt. You performed an action that caused an event which then had other effects that are open to interpretation. Can you then call letting that car merge in front of you a kindness or an altruistic act knowing it could have caused a negative ripple? That is just something to consider about the actions we take.

Still, I suggest doing all you can to insert kindness into the world around you because it feels good for at least you and those you know it affects. Take a few moments to talk to or help someone. You might be the best thing that happened to that person today. Just as important, you may feel appreciated and noticed and a bit more human.

We are all connected, so give yourself that great feeling by putting a smile on another's face. Don't feel guilty for wanting a reward; be grateful that those rewards come by helping to elevate others.

Worry

"I am an old man and have known a great many troubles,
but most of them never happened."
—Mark Twain

Since you are reading these words, I will assume you are presently alive, which verifies that most of your worries never came to pass.

The most freeing thought is that we are never safe. Once you recognize and accept that you were never truly safe, you can also see that you were never in as much danger as you thought. You learn to appreciate all the wonderful things that are protecting you when you lose the illusion of safety.

Seers and Charlatans

Worry is our ego telling us that we are capable of predicting the future. To a certain extent, we are indeed capable of predicting or imagining the future, but only to a very limited extent. Unfortunately, we often exaggerate to ourselves how well we can do this and how well we have done it in the past. If you honestly think back to things you worried about and the 100 different scenarios you imagined, you may have accurately predicted the future, but you were incorrect 99 of those 100 times. Your ego will think that you got it right because of that one scenario and forget about or ignore the other 99. Since logically you could not have prepared for all 100 scenarios, and you could not have accurately predicted which one of the 100 would come to pass, you were essentially incorrect; you really had no idea which outcome would come to pass. This puts you in exactly the same place as if you hadn't worried at all or only used your mental and physical energy to generally prepare for possible issues without attaching yourself to any of them.

Once we accept that we are poor predictors of the future, we can let go of trying to worry about it. Worry itself sometimes becomes the biggest problem. Worry has never altered the outcome of an event. Have you ever heard anyone say, "I'm so glad I worried about that, it really helped!"?

The actual event or outcome will be influenced by many factors that we don't even know to include when trying to predict it. An outcome will occur whether or not we have worried about it. Preparing for an outcome is useful, of course, but only as a general tool. I can prepare for a disaster by having extra water and extra food that can be prepared without electricity, but that doesn't require that a specific event or outcome like a hurricane, earthquake, or power outage take place. I don't attach to any event by trying to predict which one will require me to use those resources. I just keep myself generally safe.

The philosopher Alan Watts joked about how you can never know all the factors in a situation, so in the end you think for however long about what to do and then make what is essentially a snap decision anyway. He said this as a joke, but I see a lot of truth in it. Think of a situation in your past and imagine both a best-case and worst-case scenario of how it could have gone. (Feel free to exaggerate when doing this!) You will see the actual outcome was somewhere in the middle of those two extremes. The actual outcome could have been different in many ways for reasons known and unknown; seemingly unrelated factors could have altered it. Now apply this to a situation you have at present or pending in the future. Think about it for as long as you like; come up with a thousand possible outcomes. Any of those or something else entirely could be the actual outcome, but you won't know till you get there. It may end up as a problem or a blessing; most likely it will be both!

Worries are not something we can do anything about because they aren't things and don't have solutions. They are thoughts. We *can only* do something about and react to actual events because they are real.

Speaking of telling the future, one thing about your future is very clear... Your future self is a jerk and will admonish anything you do now. Just like your present self is a jerk to your past self.

Say you start a business today and make $1,000,000. That sounds pretty good right? Not so much to your future self, they will look at the choices you made and see where if you had done it differently that you could have made $2,000,000.

The reason this is great is that it relieves you of the mental trap that cycles you through all the possible decisions and worrying over if you are making the best decision. The simple answer is that you are absolutely not making the best decision. Now that you already know your decision is not going to be the best one, you are free, free to make a good decision and move forward. Your future self has already judged you as doing a bad job, so leave that jerk with something fun to ponder. They are going to be a jerk no matter what but they might appreciate if you leave them with a less stress addled body and mind, or they might see how you could have left them with and even more clear mind and body. There is just no way to win this one, so let it go and be free knowing that even your best is already a mistake.

But What If?

Is there any advice you would give to your younger self?

Me: "Nope, I know he made it this far"

A similar thought pattern to worry is playing the "What if" game, as in "What if I had done ___ instead?" Again, you are trying to predict the future, but in this scenario, you are relying on a different past in an alternate universe. This will get you into incomprehensible black holes of mental energy waste. What if things happened exactly how they needed to for you to learn a skill that will prevent future disaster or make you a stronger person? What if the other event had occurred and an unknown factor came into play that made the outcome even worse?

This is a problem of imagination; what you imagine feels real to the body as if it had actually happened. You feel the rush of adrenaline, an increase in cortisol production that has a negative effect on your organs. Your heart rate and blood pressure go up. You are causing harm to your body because of something that doesn't yet exist and maybe never will. If you worry too much about getting sick or dying, you may be hastening that very outcome.

Fear vs. Worry

We often lump fear in with worry and anxiety, but fear is about something real. While explaining the difference to a friend, I suddenly lunged forward and yelled "AHHHH!!" in his face. "That is fear," I said about his reaction. I went on to explain that worry and anxiety are what you are now experiencing while wondering what terrible thing I will do next to illustrate worry. Maybe you think I will yell again or do something worse. Perhaps you tense up in anticipation of these imagined scenarios. What are you doing? You are worrying, you are trying to predict the future. That is worry, it is nothing but imagination and ego working together to accomplish nothing.

Fear = A tiger running toward you.

Worry = There might be a tiger behind that bush.

One is a clear and definite problem that needs your attention; the other becomes a problem only if you let it. If there are signs pointing to a tiger behind the bush, prepare for that outcome by avoiding the bush. Planning and preparing can help a lot by making you feel like you have done all you can to elicit the best outcome from the situation. Fear, on the other hand, is a useful tool that causes you to react when that tiger is running toward you. Fear causes you to hit the brakes when the car in front of you slams on theirs or throw up your hands when someone tries to punch you. Fear is reserved for an immediate danger you need to react to.

Worry has never altered the outcome of an event; the outcome will be what it will be whether you spent your energy worrying or walking through a beautiful park. Worry gets you in trouble when you spend more energy on it than dealing with an actual problem or knowing when to walk away from something you have no control over. Save that energy for the actual event, either to deal with the problem or to celebrate the victory.

The Worry Matrix

The mental, emotional, and physical toll that worry takes will absolutely become a problem. If you want something to worry about, worry about being worried!

I write this book from an area that gets hurricanes and tornadoes. Will my worry about a tornado injuring me or destroying my home prevent that tornado? I do like to feel empowered, but thinking my imagination will stop a hurricane might be pushing my limits. Chances are strong it will not hit my house, but there's a definite chance that those worries will negatively affect my health.

The worry matrix looks like this:

- I worried and a tornado hit my house resulted in 2 problems
- I worried and a tornado did not hit my house resulted in 1 problem
- I did not worry and a tornado hit my house resulted in 1 problem
- I did not worry and a tornado did not hit my house resulted in 0 problems

You can use this simple worry matrix with anything; the results will always be the same. The instances where you do not create additional problems will always lead to fewer problems.

This different way of thinking about worry is not something that happens overnight. Worry slips into my mind all the time; so do fantasies of perfect life scenarios. It's a matter of practice. Each time a worry comes up, ask yourself if it will help or change that potential scenario. Since you can only think of one thing at a time, use this logic to diminish the power of the worry, then think of the best case scenario or the beach.

Your ego will tell you that you must worry in order to make a plan. But a plan for what? A plan for something that may not happen? That seems like a strange use of your time. Yes, it is good to make plans, but since you cannot know the details of an outcome, obsessing over a detailed plan is just going to be wasted energy. Remember: When you make these plans, you are also making plans for someone who does not yet exist. By the time that plan may be needed, you will be a different person and may no longer like it. Keep plans general and use only a little of your precious time and energy.

And whenever you feel a desire to imagine the future, I highly recommend having the most fun you can by only imagining best-case scenarios.

Cats and Lawnmowers

I was walking my cat Scribbles on his leash and the local landscapers were working nearby with a loud lawnmower. They walked the lawnmower toward where my cat and I were chilling and watching the world. My first instinct was to worry that as they got closer, it would frighten the cat and he would panic and try to run. I went through the whole scenario in my head. Will he break away from his leash? Will he be afraid of going outside in the future? Will there be claws flying everywhere? Will he get hurt or become lost?

It turned out the only negative outcome was my anxiety. The cat simply laid quietly and watched with mild curiosity as the obnoxious lawnmower rumbled by. The man pushing it smiled and nodded as he passed. I was the only creature in that scene who had a bad time.

I already knew everything I needed to know in case something happened. The cat was on a leash so I could likely prevent escape. I am well practiced at grabbing and holding him when something scares him. I knew that whatever happened, I would respond with whatever my current capacity was in that moment. I should have no need to worry and put myself into a worse mental state with a lower capacity to respond effectively than if I was calm and not worried. In fact, I could have created multiple problems for myself by being worried. Scribbles could have sensed my fear which may have triggered him to panic.

And there would have been no reason to feel guilty had there been an incident of panic. Should I then never walk my cat because of what might happen in the future? Do I still go for walks but ruin the joy with worry at every corner? Or should I have faith in my preparations and enjoy the moment? Walks are one of the things that bring us both great joy and are worth the potential risks.

Expect Nothing – Be Prepared for Anything

Let's say your boss calls you into their office. You have no idea why. Maybe you made a mistake. If so, it's already done; the consequences of that mistake will be what they are whether you worry or not. Perhaps they just want your opinion on what color to use for the background of a presentation or to thank you for always bringing joy and peace to the office. If you spent any time worrying after getting that call, it served absolutely no purpose except to disrupt thoughts that could have been productive.

If you already think you know what the issue is, then you already know what happened and hopefully how to prevent it happening again. Worry won't add to the conversation or help in the cleanup. In fact, it is more likely to just get in the way of a real conversation about the issue. But again, maybe they just want to ask how your pet fish Harry is doing . . .

"But what if I can't pay my mortgage?" Then something else will happen. Maybe to your liking, maybe not. You really can't know or control what that will be, and the possibilities are quite limitless, from "Everyone dies in a nuclear explosion" to "Your payment is late by a week and then you win the lottery." But what if you *can* pay your mortgage and you were worried about it anyway? Now you paid the mortgage and, by worrying, you paid a toll on your soul, mind, and body. Did you come out ahead? Did worry pay part of the mortgage for you?

Another common worry is running out of money. I've had this worry many times, so I know it well. The truth is, you will either run out of money or you won't. Yes, this sounds oversimplified, but it's the truth and worrying about it won't change the outcome. It will only waste energy that you could be using to come up with solutions. Perhaps you could develop a second income like becoming a social media influencer or delivering pizzas. Maybe you need a new job. Where does "I'm worried about finding a new job" go on your resume?

Stressing over how well you did on a test you took while you wait for the test results is another waste of energy. You already made the effort to study and take the test. Now it's done. The results won't change whether you worry yourself into a panic or go to the park and lay in the nice, warm grass. Since the result will be the same either way, choose a more productive way to spend the time.

Increased confidence is a bonus side effect of reduced worry and anxiety. We often worry if people will like us or not. The more confident we are, the more likely they are to like us. When we worry if they will like us, they will see a nervous person and are less inclined to see us in a favorable light. People will like you or they won't, so you might as well be your true self and attract people who like you for that rather than the mask you may be presenting them with – which is what we really want anyway. We forget that when we do not know someone the starting point is them not liking us. How could they like us till they know us? This means you start at 'they don't like you' and it can only get more positive from there. And besides, there are billions of people in the world. We only see the few we interact with regularly, incorrectly thinking they are our only chance to have friends and allies. But among those billions are also many people who will appreciate you for exactly who you are.

Our brains developed when we lived in small tribes, the tribe was our only safety and ostracization meant death, so we had to be liked. This is where that worry and anxiety about being liked comes from. Today we live around an abundance of people and our safety is not as tied to a particular group because there are many options for groups.

Many of us experience crushing social anxiety and the fear of being embarrassed. This fear assumes that other people think or care as much about you as you do. They don't. Consider how many people you interact with during a day. If you think about them at all, it is usually quite brief and only about what they might have thought of you and less about what they did or told you. Even if you do remember them, you are at best remembering just a tiny piece of who they are – as they do of you. The key to not worrying about a social interaction is to remember that people live in their own worlds with little concern for what you do unless the interaction with you becomes a major event in their life.

The true you that lives below the worrying is what will attract great and compatible people into your life. Less worry = the best friendships.

Stress

"There is more to life than increasing its speed."
— Mahatma Gandhi

OMG! If I don't get all this done, then [insert something terrible] will happen! This is an example of worry, not stress. Stress is not accepting that we can only do one thing at a time and overestimating how long something will take to do. Making the distinction is important so you are working on the right problem. Taking medicine for a headache is unlikely to fix your upset stomach.

Multitasking Is a Lie

The world is going faster and faster and getting more intense. Keeping pace with an ever-changing news cycle and multiple events that come and go is a growing challenge. How can you stay on top of it all and keep your conversations fresh with the people you meet or hang out with?

Here's a tip: Don't think about things until it's time to think about them. If you start too early, you are making presumptions about what the future will be and may need to change your conclusions. If you think about things too late, you will make yourself suffer for events that cannot be changed. Similar to taking actions, you only get to focus on one thought at a time, so if a thought isn't immediately useful, think of something that is.

We spend so much time stressing about how long it will take to do all the things on our list that we need to start factoring in the time we spend stressing about how long it will take.

- Do dishes take an hour? Probably not. I can do a sink full of dishes in less than 15 minutes.
- I can vacuum the house in 20 minutes. This is only about 1% of my day.
- I can cook a meal in 10 to 30 minutes. I might play an educational podcast while I do it.
- Cleaning the litter box only takes a couple of minutes, but once it's done, I feel better about having a happy cat.

We have a lot of time in the day, and we often spend it thinking about or avoiding our list of tasks instead of just picking one and getting it out of the way.

No matter what your task is at the moment or how many times you are pulled in another direction, just remember that you can only do one thing at a time and you are doing this task right now. Other tasks can be given attention when it's their turn. Thinking about another task while you are working on the present one only sucks energy from the current task. You will get through the current task faster by focusing on it, then you will get through the next task faster by giving it the attention it deserves. The total time for both tasks and the quality of results of each task will be improved, simply by relaxing.

Slow Down

You can do more with a calm mind at a slow pace than with an excited mind trying to do everything at once. There is research showing that people who walk slower and drive slower are happier. They take the time to appreciate what is around them or think about how to best handle something. They don't make as many errors or lose time having to fix those errors while handling new and unfinished projects.

I watch people from my new perspective and see how I used to be when I would try to rush through life. I used to walk very fast. I would drive aggressively. This put a feeling of intensity into everything I did, and intensity is exhausting! When you drive fast, you feel you are running out of time, you feel the pressure and stress, your brain says you must be short on time because you are driving fast. When you drive and walk slower, you feel like there's time to get everything done because why else would you be moving at such a relaxed pace? It is a magical and counter-intuitive thing that happens: By going slower, you manage to get more done at a faster pace. You put yourself into a place where you choose to focus on just one thing, and that calm focus allows you to be more productive.

When we are moving too fast, the feedback we get from our brain says that we must be in the midst of an emergency or why else would we be running around like this. When we are in the middle of an emergency, we release stress hormones like cortisol and adrenaline. This makes the body move even faster, which tells the brain to keep the hormones coming. Taking a moment to align and settle down breaks this loop and allow us to think in a more calm and focused manner. Observe the muscles in your face and body, relax the ones that are trying to tense up. This will tell your brain that the emergency has ended, you can return to normal functioning.

Some have social anxiety where the trained reaction is to try and speed through social interactions. When we do this, it reinforces to our brain that social interaction is dangerous. It must be, because we are moving quickly and trying to escape, right? Why else would we be rushing except to avoid danger? The trick is to intentionally make any social interaction last longer and be as slow about it as we can.

Consider a person who has anxiety over going to the store. They will rush in, keep their heads down to avoid others, throw some items in their cart, and get the hell out. Everything about that tells the brain "I am going to die!". Instead walk slowly into the store and through it, leave your phone in your pocket, keep your head up and smile softly at everyone you encounter or pass, spend an extra moment considering the options for each item, get in the longest checkout line, while waiting look up at the store beyond the up close magazines and gum, smile at the person behind you, appreciate all that goes into making the store what it is with all these amazing products, then say something fun to the cashier, and finally walk slowly out of the store. You can do this with any social situation or interaction. It tells your brain there is absolutely nothing to fear. How could I walk so slowly and take everything in if my life were in danger? That makes no sense, so I must be safe. I can relax and enjoy the world around me, simply by going slower and reinforcing to my whole being that there is no danger.

The feeling of hurry also reduces your empathy for others because you don't have time to feel it. That slower person in front of you becomes your enemy because it seems they are working against you. When you slow down your pace and see someone moving fast or being aggressive, you have the time and freedom to think of how difficult it must be for them to go through their day feeling that way. You even appreciate the slow person in front of you for reminding you to take the time to look around and enjoy all that you are in the presence of. When my goal is to get someplace quickly, I see anything between me and that goal as an obstacle. I don't see a person; I see someone "in my way." Instead of seeing the great work that went into placing the bricks of the sidewalk, I just speed by, barely looking. When moving fast, I miss the smell of the flower bed, the soft feel of the gentle breeze, or the happy dog who wants attention. These and an infinite number of other things to be grateful for slip right past us. I invite you to catch just a few more of them each day.

Be polite and considerate when driving to make being polite and considerate the norm. While this will not have an immediate effect and in some cases may even annoy people who are trying to be aggressive, it will, in the long run, help normalize politeness which is desperately needed in our society. Take a moment to imagine what may be going on in the life of the person ahead of you causing delays. You will find this opens you up to seeing the world as a friendlier place. These are not your enemies; they are people like you who are doing their best to get through the day.

Smile at the person who is paying with a check in the express lane at the grocery store. Say hello to the cats, dogs, and children you encounter and give them a moment of your time. Appreciate the shape of the cracked cement you step on or the leaves of the tree as you walk under it. Allow yourself to pause for a moment; it won't affect your schedule to be a few seconds later getting to your destination, but your heart and soul will thank you.

Work Hard to Work Harder

Stress has a cost; it comes in the form of mental and physical destruction. It also has the cost of trying to reduce that destruction by buying our way out of it. We may get a job that pays twice as much but find we are spending a lot more money going out, taking more vacations, buying bigger TVs – whatever we can to help counter the stress from the higher expectations of a job that our egos think we need in order to be happy. We may say that, in order to keep and stay sane in our job, we need to spend extra money on certain things that make us feel the stress was worth it. But we can easily become stuck in this cycle, not knowing the difference between the cause and the effect. Someone with a position that pays less but is less intense, by comparison, can more easily be happy and won't need to spend as much money countering the effects of a higher-stress job and lifestyle.

People who love you wouldn't want you killing yourself at a job just to provide them a fancier lifestyle. If they do want that, you may question why you would endure such a job for people who don't mind you being destroyed for their benefit. Maybe you do this willingly, but so your ego can boast how honorable you are being or because you are truly doing it for others. If you think you are doing it for others, have you asked them directly and honestly if they prefer you working 80 hours a week and earning a huge paycheck over spending time with them? Money is a lot less fun when it smells like regret.

In many cases, the reason you work at a job you hate is because you want to be the honorable provider, or you went to school for this so you should do it, or you worked your way up the ladder so you can't just give it up, maybe you have become accustomed to a certain lifestyle that goes with your position and the wealth it brings. If you are in such a position, I can't say if it's worth it for you because I am not you. But I do suggest taking time on a regular basis to honestly think about it. You aren't the person who started that job, so you should decide if you are the person who wants to still be there and if the rewards are worth the sacrifice. If not, take appropriate action. But if you do want to be there, it's important to start treating it like the game it is...

There is little difference between work and fun except mindset. A teenage boy who wants to impress girls will spend countless hours learning to play a guitar. He will persistently move past any difficulties or obstacles. In many video games, one must do what is called "grinding" to get the higher rewards. This is happily done by many gamers all over the world, not for profit but for something they actually paid money to do! They see even the most boring work in the game as fun because their brains associate it with fun.

We can do this at work, for example, by shifting our perspective from "I have to run this report" to "I will make this financial report so good the gods will weep and tales will be told of it for generations!". There is a certain sense of joy, pride, and satisfaction that fuel the soul when we see our work this way. Maybe try some healthy and friendly competition. When I worked at a job that often felt quite oppressive, we had a way of making it a little better. It was at a call center where we spent all day taking calls and dreading each one. Sometimes the queue would back up, and a few of us would challenge each other to see who could handle the most calls till the queue returned to normal volumes. We would have a great time and hardly be phased by upset customers or frustrating issues. The thing I failed to notice at the time was that if we had done that *all* day, the job would not have felt oppressive.

When you take pride in and find joy in everything you do, you'll be rewarded with feelings of satisfaction and happiness. It takes a little practice but I promise it is worth it! We sometimes get embarrassed by wanting to do a good job at work because it's normal to hate what you do and become exhausted by each task your manager gives you. Instead of, "I have to write this report" or "I have to help this difficult customer", to "I get to learn more about the data that goes into this report" and "Here's a chance to increase my capacity to deal with a difficult person so the next difficult person will be easier."

Do the right thing

Your future self is a jerk. Just like your present self is a judgmental jerk to your past self. But this can be a good thing! No matter how well you did in the past your present self can look back and say, "Well, you could have done ___ better". Even if you started a company that made 2 million dollars, your present self will say, "Yeah, but you could have made 3 million if you had ___". This means that whatever you are doing now will be judged harshly by your future self, no matter how well you are doing or how smart your present decisions are. When it comes to the stress of making decisions or taking actions this can be very freeing and helpful. Once you accept you will be judged harshly, you no longer need to worry about that judgement. It will be harsh no matter the outcome. You can simply and freely act to the best of your present ability.

"Do the right thing." This is what I like to tell my teams. If you do what you think is right, you will always be able to justify what you did and why. You will take pride in your actions because they were to the best of your ability. This can apply to work or life in general. You may not be correct. We all make mistakes, so whenever you take an action that you think is the right thing to do, you'll feel better about what you did (even if the task is distasteful) and have an honest explanation of why you did it. If it turned out to be a mistake, you can still hold your head high. You won't be acting like prey so others will be less inclined to assume the predator role toward you and instead they will be more understanding and forgiving.

Feel free to step away from something rather than make immediate decisions that your ego will attach itself to. Once your ego attaches to a decision or direction, you will find yourself justifying it even if it's not the best or correct path. This is true in all aspects of life, not just at work. Consider a disagreement with someone where you take a stand/side on an issue, choosing what house or car to buy, hearing a news report and reacting without more complete evidence, even whether or not you like someone. It is well known that we react emotionally and often make a decision in that state, then our brains will jump through all sorts of hoops to rationalize and maintain that position through any evidence. We will in fact ignore and discount counter evidence so that we can maintain our treasured position, no matter how objectively incorrect it may be.

In most workplaces, when meetings take place, everyone wants a decision before the meeting is over. We put our energy into making that happen instead of taking enough time to let our thoughts process into the best decision. Then we find we have identified with a direction or decision, it in a way becomes who we are. The ego says "I agreed to that so it must be right" then the brain works to justify why it is right despite new evidence, because the ego sees change and being wrong as a type of death.

We might then end up working in a direction that is not ideal because we identified with it too quickly. Often, the decision is strongly influenced by the most charming or manipulative person in the room. They may or may not intend to influence us this way, but it can and does happen. Stepping away, taking time to consider, allows us to think more clearly in our own way, remaining open and flexible to other ideas while avoiding a premature attachment. Allow yourself to take time to do the right thing in the first place or realize when the right thing means changing direction. Identify with doing the right thing as who you are and little things like decisions and direction changes will not feel like death to the ego.

Mental Debt

There is a method for paying off debts where you pay the smallest one first and then once that is paid off, you move to what is now the smallest debt. With each debt you pay off, you free up more resources to pay off the next one. This applies not just to money but also to how we use – and use up – our mental energy. I use this method for stress reduction in both my personal and work life.

When I start my day, I organize in the following manner:

- Take care of things I can handle right now such as someone asking for a "yes or no" reply. I no longer use my mental energy on these.
- Handle any true emergency as it exists or comes up.
- Send questions or tasks to others; the sooner they get them, the sooner I'll hear back.
- Prioritize issues by how many people are affected or how much money is affected (often these mean the same thing).
- Let people know an ETA on any longer-term issues I'm responsible for.
- Depending on deadlines, handle smaller projects first to get them off my plate.

Now that most of my plate is clear, I can more easily focus on larger and ongoing projects as I have the time and attention to make sure they are delivered with the best quality and thought. Any action makes a difference, even if it only moves the project 2%. That's 2% you no longer need to think about.

Intoxication Reverberation

Some things we do to relieve stress become causes of our stress. I am referring mostly to drugs and alcohol, but this applies to any unhealthy vice. Let's be honest though, I am mostly speaking of alcohol because it is the most destructive to the individual and the society, yet ironically is the most culturally accepted. I am going to take you down an unusual path to offer a view of intoxication you may not have heard before.

First, we are all familiar with the idea that alcohol is a crutch that causes the 'muscles' used to deal with situations in a healthy manner to atrophy, and with that it gives us false happiness, also known as pleasure. We rob ourselves of the truly deep pride and joy that come from strength and personal growth. We accept this momentary pleasure in trade for the long lasting joy we could experience, we then keep refilling our glass with alcohol in order to recharge that short lived pleasure instead of working on true unbreakable happiness that refills itself from the joy of life. Often that constant joy from life seems non-existent because we have thrown it in a hole and kicked dirt over it for years. We have often prevented ourselves from learning the proper coping mechanisms, our first instinct on a bad day(or even a good day) is to reach for a drink or other intoxicant instead of working through the problem.

I did say I would speak of less common, but I think more important, reasons we will want to avoid intoxication. So, let's start with the why...

One method of losing the desire for alcohol is to ask yourself why you want a drink. I will list some of those 'whys' and how they can lead you down a path of self-discovery. I find that when I truly understand the 'why' of doing something like drinking, I won't want to do it anymore.

- "I drink to relax or loosen up"
  - Why can I not relax without drinking?
    - Because I keep thinking about my problems - See my chapter on worry and anxiety
    - Because there is so much going on - Does the alcohol help you resolve any of those to get them off your plate?
- "I like to drink"
  - Why do I like to drink?
    - Because it helps me avoid uncomfortable feelings – Wouldn't you do better to handle those rather than poison yourself and add more problems?

- Because I like the way it feels – What can I do to like the way sober feels?

- "I Like the flavor"
  - Why is it when you drank for the first time it was nasty?
    - Be honest with yourself, alcohol tastes terrible and you like the intoxication, but liking the intoxication sounds way less classy. You acquired a taste for that nasty stuff because you like the way it helps you avoid the harder work of self-improvement

- "I drink to be social"
  - Why can I not be social without it?
    - Do I have a fear of making a fool of myself and want to be able to blame alcohol? Drinking increases your foolishness, creating the problem you wanted to avoid
    - Do I not like the people I am trying to be social with? – That should tell me something about my life choices and people I am around – Do I really want to fit in with people my inner being is screaming at me to avoid?

165

In all cases you will find there is something about yourself or your life that you are trying to cover up and avoid dealing with. These are things in the psychological shadow that you are trying to repress and hide because they are painful to honestly deal with, areas of your life where your true self is screaming for you to do something different, or places where you can regrow those atrophied 'muscles' of true and honest happiness.

Alcohol devalues life. If you had 1 hour to live, you would want to be as present as possible to take in every moment of that hour. That hour would be the most precious thing you have ever experienced. At what point does an hour become of no value or decreased value? When does gold become garbage? Each hour is the most precious thing you will ever have, they are all gold, none are garbage.

The subconscious mind thinks differently than our conscious mind. It understands us saying life is not valuable when we drink, if life is not worth being present for here and now, then why would it suddenly become worthy of our attention and full presence other times? The subconscious hears us saying that life itself is not valuable. That means all life loses value. To the subconscious which is making many of our decisions for us through desires, our own life is not worth treasuring, so we act in ways that disrespect ourselves, our value, and our time. Along with that devaluing of self we also lose respect for the value of other lives and end up devaluing and dehumanizing others. This represents itself in encouraging poor behavior from ourselves and those around us. The sad part is we do not even see it as bad or inappropriate behavior because we have devalued life in general in our conscious minds. But here we have dissonance causing us unhappiness, anger, and projections of our shadow because our true selves know that we have devalued ourselves, our friends, our families, and even our children.

Being intoxicated also tells those around us they are not worth our full presence or we do not wish to be around them. If the real me wanted to be around someone I would want to fully be in their presence and be fully present for the interaction. Why would I want to miss a moment with a loved one? Why would I only want to be partially there for someone I considered important? Now think of it from the perspective of their higher self, they see that you do not want to be present with them and whether the conscious mind sees it or not the feelings of their higher self have been affected. On some level they understand your lack of desire to truly be present with them. When you have a couple or even friends that drink together this becomes a feedback loop where each sees the other avoiding them, which increases their own desire to be less present so they drink more, cycle repeats.

Drinking also puts into a feedback loop of weakness. When I get intoxicated rather than dealing with whatever inspired me to drink, I tell myself I am too weak to deal with that issue. Oh, but not just that issue. Remember the subconscious mind is different, what it hears is I am too weak to deal with issues. Yes, all issues. Each drink says, "I am weak". Weak animals in nature are prey, prey animals have more stress than the strong predators. Prey looks around for everything that is after it so they can run. When you drink you are turning yourself into that stressed out and weak prey animal. This causes you to turn to alcohol to hide from that weakness, cycle repeats. They say alcohol gives one courage, but in reality, it robs you of strength and courage by preventing you from ever truly attaining them in your life. I could drink and go talk to that cute girl or I could just go talk to her. Consider the real positives and negatives of both scenarios. In one she never really meets me nor I her and in the other we like or dislike based on reality. In both cases one runs the chance of looking like a fool, but more is learned from acting a fool based on your true self than from acting a fool as a diminished self. The power is where the blame is, do you want the power, or do you want the alcohol to have it?

There is an absurdity to paying money for something that kills us physically, mentally, and socially. You are paying money to devalue yourself, your time, your loved ones, and your health.

The Ultimate Stress Reliever

Smile more. Seriously, the best way to counter stress is to smile. Smile at someone and make their day better. When they smile back, there are now two extra smiles in the world whether at home or work or walking down the sidewalk. Make it a habit. Make it normal. The more smiles there are, the less stress there will be.

Grief

"What we have once enjoyed deeply we can never lose.
All that we love deeply becomes a part of us."
–Helen Keller

Fall in love with grief, for at the heart of grief is the purest love of all. When you fall in love with grief, you remove the fear and the hatred that often comes with it . This lessens its power and control over you. When you understand grief, you will learn to be grateful for it.

Grief and Love are Memory

At the heart of grief is love – love for memories. Because memories are all we have of a person. I fall in love with someone or something because of the effect they had on me and the strong emotion it created within me. That event or those events that led to my love are all memories, and those memories remain whether or not their source is physically present in my life. I still have what I had when they were with me.

When a loved one passes, you can feel gratitude for all the memories you still have of them. They are the same memories you had while they were here. Even when you are sitting next to someone enjoying their presence and watching a lovely sunset. I remember the good times we had at the state fair, the lovely way they treated a waiter, the help they gave when I was hurt, and so many other events we went through together. I remember the way they smell or feel right now because we are always living slightly in the past. You experience and interpret very recent memories as the present. Because our brains process everything from the world, the delay created means we are always in the past, in memories of experience. To us and even our bodies, there is little difference between reality and imagination or between experience and memory. I can still 'experience' a lost event or person by remembering.

The memories of something are all we ever have and all we ever had. When I'm sitting next to someone I care about, Those memories cause us to feel emotions for someone whether they are with us or not.

You haven't lost them; what you've lost is your story or predictions about what future feelings or memories that loved one would bring you. Since we couldn't tell the future when we were with them or now that they are gone, we cannot know what would have come or is to come. But we are able to reach into the past via those memories and experience whatever joyous feelings those memories brought at the time or what they bring us now. Again, this is precisely what we did when they were still alive and present in our lives. I do not experience crippling grief for the loss of my still living cat 'Max' when I run to the store, because he still exists within me.

When we lose someone or something we hold dear in our hearts, it feels devastating because it's like a black hole has been created in the fabric of space and time. Someone or something important has been removed from existence and we grieve because we have an amazing capacity to love. Fortunately, we get to keep that capacity to love as well as the memories of that which is no longer with us. The grief is a reminder of who you are as a loving person and a chance to appreciate your capacity for that love. The greater level to which you accept that capacity the more you know you can have that love and appreciation for everything you remember in your life, be it a memory from now or long ago.

Haunted by the Living

Feeling the presence of one who is no longer with us means your mind is using the memories of them to predict what they would normally do or what they would do now that they are no longer here.

This also happens when they are still in our lives. Sometimes we think someone is in the room with us or sitting in their favorite spot only to find, when we look again, that they are not there. How many times have you asked an empty room a question thinking the other person was still there only to find that they had left? Have you ever felt a pet walking across your legs in bed at night only to remember they had passed away, or are still alive but in the other room?

I like to relate this to the idea of seeing ghosts. Maybe ghosts are real and maybe not. The point is, sometimes people see them. Your brain spends a lot of time predicting and making up what it sees as the next likely event, because this is far more efficient and faster than trying to process everything in real time. You often know how someone is going to end a sentence because your brain knows what words are likely to come next, like the predictive text on a phone. If you notice, you often get a little disoriented when what they say does not follow the expected pattern. This is how comedy works, you expect the idea to go down a certain path, and then you experience surprise and humor when it takes a different route than your brain predicted. When you go into a 'haunted' house you may see someone walking down the hall, because that is what people do in halls. Your brain sees a hall and makes a prediction of someone doing what they do, walking down it. That gets processed from 'that is what might happen here' into that is what is happening here.

Whether someone is physically with us or not, alive or not, we are able to think of what they would say, how they would like a particular event, what they would order at a restaurant, where they would prefer to sit, and many other things about them. We have a construction of them in our minds made up of memories which make up our feelings about them.

I can predict what a loved one will order at the restaurant whether they are sitting next to me, across town, or after they've been gone for 20 years. That part of them is in me and with me. They aren't gone because they influenced who you are, and that influence will never leave you. Aspects of them will continue to live on through you and others. Remember: we become like those we spend the most time around and those who have the greatest influences on our lives, just as they take on aspects of us from the time they spend in our presence, we blend together in a way. We become them, we keep that part of them no matter where they are or what state of being they are in.

If you have ever asked yourself what a lost loved one would say or do, and your predictions turn out to be correct? That is them with you and within you. How else could you possibly do this? With people who are alive, we can later confirm that our prediction was correct because we can witness them taking the predicted action. We are quite often correct in our prediction, telling us they are with us in our minds and hearts, whenever we need them, alive or after they have passed. Do we miss holding them and caring for them? Having coffee with them in the morning? We can do this through our memories.

Think of gatherings that reflect on the life of a lost loved one. This group of people were all influenced in some way by that person and each adds a piece of the person so that together the group has brought that lost loved one back into its presence. Your piece of your experience of them, how they influenced your life, is added to the pieces the other people carry. This doesn't speak of an absence but to a presence that you are blessed to keep as long as it serves you. They will always be part of you; they will be there whenever you need them.

Grief can be used as a reminder to spend more time around those who are important to you so you can integrate more of who they are into who you are. It can remind you to be open with those you love and allow them to be open with you so you can better know their true being and carry that with you. Being open with others is also how you can live on through your memories of them or, while alive, truly be a part of their lives. Allow yourself to become even more like them, so that much more of them is carried with you.

You may experience the death of a loved one as a death that happens inside you. It is an event you experienced but the reason it bothers you is because of all the other events that made their existence so wonderful for your life.

There is a beautiful poem called "The Rainbow Bridge" that says you will meet a departed love one again and walk across the rainbow bridge together. I love this poem and suggest that you take a moment to feel that you are walking right now on the rainbow bridge not just with those who have passed but those who are currently in your life and, well, everyone on the planet. We are all walking across the bridge to eternity together simply by interacting and filling the feedback loops that connect us.

Grief is such a beautiful emotion because the stronger you feel it, the more wonderful the reasons you were given to feel it. Connect more deeply with more people and you will have plenty of reasons to feel both love and grief. It's okay to smile and cry at the same time. The feeling of doing both can be a freeing experience that turns grief into gratitude.

They Don't Want You to Suffer

Over-identification with grief can be a terrible burden. Your departed loved ones would not want you to define yourself by the sadness of their absence.

Think of the pure love behind your grief and assume the one you lost felt that same pure love for you. Would someone who loves you that much want you to spend one minute being sad, or would they want you to have a beautiful, happy, joy-filled existence?

A person working a tough job that has negative mental and physical side effects to support their family will often do so gladly, because they love supporting those who love them. The same person being told by their family they need to work harder so they can have a nicer house or fancier cars will start to question if that family really loves them or if they just love the money they bring in. A loving family would see their provider hurting and would gladly accept a less extravagant lifestyle in order to save the person they love. Would you want to work hard and destroy yourself for someone who did not care about your health? I would hope not.

This is the same when it comes to the passing of a loved one. Would you want to feel crippling grief for someone who would want or expect you to feel crippling grief? I would not want anyone I care for to suffer after my passing. Just like the person working the job to provide for their family, they may choose to do it, but the loving family would not want that and would prefer they did not suffer.

From the perspective of each being, they live an eternity. When someone dies, we need not feel sorry for them because they spent an eternity on this earth, and we were lucky enough to have shared some of it.

When someone is telling me about a loved one who has passed, I often feel joy for them. A smile comes over my face because I see the love they are feeling and expressing in their sadness. I cannot help but think how fortunate they are to have had such a wonderful experience with another being.

Do you deny that you are going to die? Spoiler alert: You are going to die. Once you accept that inevitability, you need not fear anything you do. Death will come one way or the other, so why not choose to enjoy life? The worst-case scenario is that you die having fun! I don't mean to act recklessly but to accept death as the thing that makes each moment of life something to be grateful for. If we lived forever, there would be no motivation to start anything new or leave a legacy we can be proud of. Death is what makes life valuable.

We are sometimes afraid to love because love and joy can lead to future grief. Once we accept grief as an expression of and continuation of that love and joy, we can allow ourselves to love more often and more deeply. The loss of an important love can feel world-shattering, of course, but there are hopefully other loves in your life and others still to be found. A good friend of mine lost his wife and felt that interest in another woman would be a disservice to his lost wife. That's understandable. We often need time to experience our grief to honor the loved one we lost, but that loved one would also want you to move on. Remember: You may have lost the loved one, but you haven't lost the love. Nor would those who have gone want you to.

We will never find another love like the one we lost because our relationship with that person was unique. The fact that you have enough love to grieve says that you have enough to find another love that is just as good. And don't avoid love because one day it will come to an end. The love doesn't need to end even when someone has left us.

There is one more important person who doesn't want you to be sad: You. Does your present self want your future self to be sad? Would your past self want your present self to be sad? Just as you would not condemn another person to sadness, you don't want to condemn yourself to sadness.

New Identity

Over-identifying with grief or any other emotion can come to define us if we aren't careful. I can love my cat without becoming my cat. I can love my spouse without becoming them.

Perhaps grief is a part of your ego dying because you were identified with that loved one - or thing - in some manner. You are so used to patterns related to that person, your brain expects them to be there when you look in a certain place at a certain time.

If you are experiencing grief and trying to figure out who you are without the person who is gone, consider that you likely dedicated at least part of your life to them, defined yourself as part of them, and now have a chance to start again without that identity attachment. You can be anyone you want because you are a blank slate – maybe not completely blank, but it is an opportunity to get to know yourself again and start with a new perspective.

If you over-identify with the grief, you will overlook all of the other people and beings in your life that you currently love or are loved by. You also run the risk of neglecting the blessings you already have. Remembering to have gratitude and appreciation for the good things you do have in your life will help redirect all of the love energy that you're putting into the grief. Spend time with others who care about you and are important to you. Give your pet an extra treat.

When my cat Aeffchen died, I was not directly grateful for losing him, because I would love to have had him forever physically by my side. I *am* grateful that he and I were so close and that losing him hurt so much. What an amazing experience to be so close with another being! This I am grateful for. Being taught to love in such a way is a special blessing. I am grateful for the emotions that inspired me to share my thoughts in this book with you – an inspiration that came soon after my feline friend passed. Would I have shared such thoughts on happiness without such sadness? Would I have kept these thoughts to myself and gone on with life as usual without his passing? I do not know. I do know that I am grateful for the gift of this expression.

I can mourn his loss without identifying with the sadness. I can be here every day for the cat that is still with me and who remains an amazing creature. I am grateful for the chance to grow closer to my still living cat Max, because I have a deeper appreciation of what a wonderful creature he is. He was great before, but now he and I are becoming closer in a way that would not have happened while my older cat Aeffchen was still alive. Were I not coming from a place of gratitude or if I was stuck in the past, I wouldn't see and appreciate what I have now.

The more you allow yourself to love and appreciate everything around you, from a tiny flower to a passing stranger, the more love you will have in the moments where grief feels overpowering. If I have $1,000,000 and lose $10,000, I'm still ok. I may be temporarily sad for the missing money, but I still have plenty of other dollars.

The more normal you make changing your routines and patterns the easier it becomes to alter them and to accept the new patterns because we learn to lessen the attachment to those patterns. Dr. Joe Dispenza speaks a lot about how we become our patterns and our routines. Those keep us stuck traveling along a well-worn path and not seeing or accepting other paths we could take. When constantly creating and trying new patterns becomes normalized you can reduce existing grief and lessen the impact of future events that cause grief, be that for a person, job, pet, or lifestyle. One could say you learn to strongly identify with not identifying as strongly with things.

Be grateful that you have an open heart which allows you to love enough to be hurt. Hurt doesn't start with hurt; it starts with love and joy. Once you change your relationship with grief and feel the gratitude for all it brings you, it no longer has power over you. It becomes your ally. When you recognize that the grief you are feeling is an intense form of love and gratitude, the experience shifts from a feeling of oppression to one of bliss and undeniable joy.

Outcomes

"To define is to limit" —Oscar Wilde

Saying that you will be happy only when something specific happens limits your happiness, both in the present and in the future. How many opportunities for happiness are you overlooking or minimizing by focusing on just one reason for it?

Here is a story Alan Watts would tell:

There was a farmer whose horse escaped and ran into the woods.

People in the town came to the farmer and said, "We're so sorry your horse escaped. That is awful."

The farmer said, "Maybe."

The next day the horse returned and with it were seven wild horses the farmer was able to catch.

Everyone in the town exclaimed, "That is such great fortune!"

The farmer said, "Maybe"

Soon after, the farmer's son was trying to tame the horses and teach them to allow a rider. He was knocked off a horse and broke his arm in the fall.

The townsfolk very compassionately said, "We are so sorry. That is terrible."

The farmer again said, "Maybe."

A couple of days later, the emperor sent men to gather all able-bodied boys in the town for service in the army. Since the farmer's son was injured, he was not included in the group taken to become soldiers.

Of course, the people of the town said, "What great fortune that broken arm turned out to be!"

The farmer calmly said, "Maybe."

An Outcome is just One Step of Many to Come

We never really know what is to come; we cannot accurately tell the future. Relying on a particular outcome means that we will need it to happen in order to feel a particular way. There is only one event that is an official outcome, that is our death. Everything leading up to that is just a step.

By requiring a specific outcome, we close ourselves off to the many other possible outcomes that might also be positive. And what is "good," anyway? We have all had bad experiences that taught us something we later used to further our success. Was the bad experience actually bad or was it beneficial? The trick is learning to see this possibility at the time rather than waiting to see it later in your life. What if we could apply the somewhat detached view of an event that hindsight gives us to when the event is actually happening? How can a difficult event be viewed in a positive light? What can we take from it and how can we do better next time? In those difficult moments, ask, "What am I learning right now?"

I have learned to see things I do not like as fuel for a better future. When something seems bad, be it objectively bad or not, it tells me I deserve better than whatever that bad thing is. I can thank the event for reminding me that I have evolved to see I am worthy of better. It was a step and a sign, moving me toward what I do deserve.

Say your neighborhood was nice when you moved in but has now gone downhill and no longer seems like a fit for you. Has the neighborhood changed, or have you changed to see the same as now less than what you are capable and worthy of? Maybe the neighborhood has objectively gotten worse but maybe it is just a subjective change. Maybe when you moved in you had a lower opinion of your self-worth and now that you have grown and that opinion of self has expanded, you see what is present as not good enough and it becomes your motivation to move on to the next better step. If you see things as perfect, you have no motivation to reach for more or to get to that next step. In this sense, things that seem bad are really good news because they alert you to your own growth that you may have missed. Even frustration over something is a sign that your true self sees you as deserving of better than what is now.

Planning to be Mad is Mad

I am always amused when people say, "I will be so mad when…" Really? You are planning to be mad? Doesn't that mean you are already experiencing the anger in anticipation of possibly experiencing the anger? If you know it's coming, wouldn't you want to avoid that negative emotion and pick a different one? Aren't you already feeling mad, sad, or depressed based on your expectation of a possible future?

Planning to be angry allows the ego to identify with future anger, which essentially gives you no choice but to be angry in that eventuality, rather than accepting whatever emotion comes at that time. Your future self will have to deal with an emotion dictated by someone else: your past less-experienced self.

Are you even sure it will happen? This is a poor use of energy and imagination. Why would you want to plan for sadness or anger when you could just as easily plan for happiness? You have the choice to change your plan, or better yet to not use energy planning your emotions. Decide at the time of the event which emotion you feel is the most useful, it saves a lot of energy and frustration.

Planning to "be happy when" is just as weird as planning to "be sad when." Let's be honest, we aren't happy "when," we just move the goalpost to the next "when." Think of something to be grateful and happy for right now, then when whatever future manifests, do that again.

In reality, you are always choosing what will make you happy or sad. You can choose it to be something in the future or you can choose to be happy about something that is now. Or just decide to be happy. I can decide "I will be happy when I get that job" or I can say "I am happy for the smell of the rain right now." You are deciding what will make you happy either way, so why not something that is. Same goes for deciding "I will be angry if they say something mean to me," you have decided what will make you angry. Maybe you could decide it is not something that will make you angry or sad. You can decide to be happy about something instead.

Can I Have Ice Cream?

When you rely on a specific outcome, you are putting your happiness into the hands of that situation, another person, or something outside of your control. Say you decide you want chocolate ice cream; you have staked your future happiness on that specific thing. Compare that to deciding you want ice cream and you'll be happy with almost any flavor. You are still being specific, though, because you are relying on ice cream as an outcome. What if there is no ice cream on the menu but there is cake? You may be disappointed because you didn't get exactly what you wanted, but cake could have been just as good and made you just as happy. We can back it off even further by saying you've decided on dessert, but that is also a specific desired outcome. Maybe the restaurant doesn't offer dessert. That will probably make you unhappy. But maybe that's okay since it might not make you feel your best later or isn't consistent with a health goal you have. In fact, not getting dessert may turn out to be what makes you happy in the long run. If your heart was set on that outcome, you limited your options for happiness.

Events will never happen exactly as you wish or predict, so wishing for and hoping for a specific way for something to play out is probably doomed to failure. Even reducing the specificity of a desired outcome still relies on that outcome happening in some way. Being open to whatever happens in any situation, whether beneficial or negative, as it is happening or after, allows you to be content with that outcome.

The trick is allowing yourself to want or desire something so that you have the motivation to pursue it, but not closing yourself to other options. Be happy with what you have and however a situation ends up. Endeavor to look from the perspective of "future you."

We usually have some level of control over how events play out, but most outcomes depend on a greater process with a lot of moving parts. To say someone will walk up and hand me $1,000,000 requires that another person act in a particular way for that outcome to be realized. I could of course hang out where there are a lot of rich people and increase my chances of such a lucky break, but by relying on that outcome, I may miss the conversation next to me where a rich man is looking for an apprentice. We ultimately have little control over most outcomes and that is probably for the best.

Good Dog. Want a Treat?

We like to pretend we are more than animals, but in many ways, we are just like our pets. We respond to those treats. If your dog pees on the floor and you give it a treat, what are you training it to do? Similarly, we want to be careful about what we are training ourselves.

What do you do when you have a bad day? Treat yourself to a favorite food, drink, service, or pastime? If yes, then you have effectively rewarded yourself for failure. The goal is to have good days and to feel happier, right? Shouldn't we be rewarding ourselves for that? By rewarding yourself for a bad day, your subconscious assumes you want more bad days so you can have more treats and it becomes happy to oblige. This system of rewards for failure will cause you to, at least subconsciously, do things to have a bad day. You may do less than your best on a work project which draws the attention of your boss. You may not do this intentionally, but your subconscious influences you to do it so you get that reward of a cocktail or a pint of ice cream. You may be less than your best with your spouse so they get annoyed with you, making your day worse and bringing that treat one step closer.

Instead, when you have a bad day or even a bad hour, end it by doing something you would normally avoid. Clean the bathroom, mow the lawn, do the dishes, talk to the weird guy at work – anything that is generally not at the top of your list. This tells your subconscious that the outcome of a bad day is something you won't like.

Then start rewarding yourself for good days. Have a great day? Reward yourself with a nice relaxing sit on the couch doing nothing. Did you nail that project at work and get showered with praise? Great, take yourself bowling! You are now rewiring your subconscious to have more good days and interactions. Your subconscious is delighted because you are now getting two rewards: a good day and a treat at the end.

In the language of your subconscious: "This action will not get the human associated with this subconscious a treat, the associated human enjoys treats, so we will do what gets them the treat and avoid that which does not provide a treat."

Thank anything that seems negative in life for showing you that you have evolved to deserve and receive better. Do not dwell on it, simply thank it for reminding you of your worth and moving you another step closer to what you do want and see you are worthy of in life. These are not negative outcomes; they are just steps. You are not rewarding yourself for having negative events in life, you are rewarding yourself for seeing the positive message they bring you.

Perspectives

Don't compare yourself to others because there is no comparison. We have all lived different lives and have different skills. To say "My life is hard" is not really accurate because you are comparing it to someone else's life that you can't ever know. We only know the life that we are living. More than that, we all have different souls and our true selves want different things. You may think you need a house as good as someone else's, but do you really? Is that your natural instinct or do you feel that way because it's the cool thing that everyone else is doing? Do you really want that faster car or just to win the approval of others? Do you really need a bigger TV, or do you just want to feel like you are more successful by having it? Use the face alignment practice from the start of the book, to see if what you think you want is really the right thing. Simply, relax your facial muscles and allow yourself to think about the object of your desire. Allow yourself to feel what your heart is telling you through your facial muscles. Do they tighten in a way that reveals pleasure and joy or do they tell you the object is not something that fills your true desires?

When feeling down or before you get out of bed in the morning, find something (or many things) to be grateful for. If you cannot think of anything, you are being dishonest with yourself. Do you have air? Do you have clean water? Do you have a family or pets? Do you have the bed you are laying on? Do you have the ability to think these thoughts? In any given moment, you have so many things to love and be grateful for.

When you look, do you see a tree or a forest? When you just see a tree, you are thinking from a scarcity viewpoint. When you see the forest and imagine its vastness beyond what you can see, you are thinking from abundance. I find more peace when I see how much there is.

In the country, it's easier to see just how large the world is because the view is expansive and uncluttered. And even then, the world is much bigger than that or the images you see on TV. A nature program may show an expansive Savannah or a huge swath of rainforest, but they are filming just a tiny fraction of a much larger place.

In cities we see a world closed in, filled and surrounded by walls of concrete. We can, however, learn to see abundance in the city if we look at a building not just as a building but as everything that went into it: all of the engineers who designed it, all the companies that provided the materials, all of the workers who built it, all the schools that trained everyone. By imagining all that went into that building instead of just seeing a towering monolith, we start to feel the abundance and how that building provided jobs and supported families and sustained communities and helped people live a good life. If we expand that to all of the buildings we walk past, the city becomes a huge and abundant place rather than a collection of gray and brown monoliths that we would normally view as oppressive.

The End Is Just Another Step

Other than death, there is no final step or final destination.

The outcome of trying to get a particular job may be getting that job, which leads to more events such as having a wonderful time or a terrible time depending on how you feel about your coworkers and environment. You may not get that job and instead see a new job posted that is even better, but you would have ignored that posting had you gotten the original job. Now that you have the job, you may want a promotion or see each day at work as another step in a larger process. Maybe years later you want to retire, so getting the job ends up looking less like an outcome than one step of many.

There is no way to predict the future, so focusing on a specific outcome as a goal is saying you will be happy because you know how everything will play out up to and after that desired outcome. Life is a string of events and we can absolutely desire for great things to happen, but we should also be ready to accept and appreciate the outcomes we do get, because outcomes are usually just steps to other outcomes.

When we tie ourselves to a particular outcome, we run the risk of putting that goal above our principles. We all have elements of psychopathy – those that ignore our conscience. Granted, the "morals" of a psychopath are far different than those of someone reading a book from the self-help section. The question is whether we'll feel regret for ignoring our principles in pursuit of outcomes we've become attached to.

For example, it becomes easier to justify treating someone poorly if you know that doing so will grant you a future reward. It's okay to be self-serving, but we can be self-serving without being mean. But if we become dependent on a particular outcome, we may cross the moral and ethical lines we created for ourselves and our actions. We identify with the desire over the true and kind self that is in our hearts. Remember, you will always be happier when you put, "Soul over Goal".

Thinking that bad things happen to bad people leads one to assume that when something bad happens to someone, they must be a bad person. If bad things happen to you, you will think you are bad and tend to see things that happen to you as bad instead of neutral or positive.

Things happen. What we make of them or learn from them is what matters. I've gone through unfortunate events in my life that I said at the time must be because I am bad or not deserving of better. Looking back, I would not have traded a single one of them. They taught me so much and made me who I am. I don't prefer tragedies; I'd much rather experience wonderful things. But I won't forget to take full advantage of both positive- and negative-seeming events; they both can teach me and help me to grow into whoever I am meant to be next. It can be hard in the moment that something bad is happening, but if you can remember to pause and ponder the lesson you are learning and how it can help you later, you will see the event in a better light. Even a little bit of insight is sometimes just enough.

When something goes wrong, my favorite line is, "If this is the worst thing that happens to me today, I'm doing pretty well." This works on anything, from running out of bubble gum to laying in a hospital bed.

We could debate all day long what is or isn't a hard life or a good life and what we need to feel like we have a good life. Something I believe has made my life hard may be laughed off by someone else as the silliest thing they've ever heard of, while something I consider easy may feel traumatic to someone with different life experiences. Does this make one life harder than another? For each, their burden feels heavy.

When you think about your life and what it took to get to where you are and all the different ways that things could have gone much worse, you could legitimately say that you do have an easy life or a good life just for the simple fact that you are here. It has been good enough that you've been able to survive it.

You may say, "I will be happy when I'm enlightened like _____." What if you never reach enlightenment? What if you think you've become enlightened and lose the motivation to stop growing? What if "enlightenment" doesn't really exist? What if true enlightenment is full of terrible epiphanies? Think again about the farmer and his son . . .

Interacting Eternities

"You cannot do a kindness too soon, for you never know
how soon it will be too late."
– Ralph Waldo Emerson

For each of us, our lifetime is our eternity. It is the only one we know. When we interact with someone, we are interacting with their eternity. How do you want to affect it? Do you want part of your eternity to be spent ruining the eternity of another? Would you want your own eternity to be less joyous? We each get one eternity and we should respect our own by respecting that of others. It feels so much better to know that part of my eternity was spent improving the eternity for another being.

Hate and Happiness Can't Exist in the Same Place

We could have 100 conversations in a day and not even one that was real. I used to talk to people on a very safe and surface level. Even when I thought I was going deep or being open, it turned out I was still on the surface and we were both filtering through fear. That fear made me hide myself from this other person who was hiding their true self as well.

When I started taking the risk of talking to people on a deeper level and going outside of standard and safe topics, I was able to make real connections.

Sure, I made fewer connections, but the ones I did make were with people who were also willing to be open and to share who they are and what they like. I am filled with joy whenever I've assumed something about a person only to find I was almost entirely incorrect. I was first seeing their avatar and not the person behind the avatar. Discovering the user behind the screen name and persona is like being an archeologist. At first you see ruins and broken pots, then you see a vibrant world and culture.

How could you not be happier when you go from seeing small icons of people to expansive universes filled with unique hopes and dreams? People love talking about what matters to them; they love talking about what is on their mind; and they love talking about what troubles them in their life and in the world. When we think of ourselves as big and complex but reduce others to tiny boxes and assumptions (especially negative ones), we encourage contempt for them and narcissistic tendencies within ourselves.

It's easy to have empathy for people in your group or those you agree with. How about those whose opinions you dislike or who operate outside of your group? The greater and more inclusive your compassion, the happier you will feel. Your world becomes a brighter place filled with wonderful people who you can understand and appreciate.

I fully encourage people to care about those who do not care about you. It would make the world a far more amazing place if more of us did that. Care but do so without expectations; don't expect others to change and start caring about you. Just keep caring and hoping for the best for them. I love being friends with people who I disagree with or who have different points of view. It helps me to think of something I like or admire about them. Sadly, this is rarely the case in modern times.

You will also find it harder to make negative judgments about people if you have smiled at them and if they have smiled at you. It forms a connection that makes it easier to see them in a positive light. When you see someone as worthwhile, you naturally feel happier, the interaction will be more positive, and you will both be making the world a better place. Remember: Life is about feedback loops. Every smile you put into the system adds to the goodness of the output.

Understand Them

I've discovered that I am least happy when stagnant and most happy when growing. When we easily identify with an idea or decision, we will fight the gods themselves to maintain that viewpoint rather than be open to being wrong as a vehicle of growth and change. Put simply, you can only grow when you are wrong. You can fight to be right, or you can allow yourself to grow.

People will shut someone out who speaks against their long-held or firm beliefs. When we deny a truth, we cause dissonance, which creates a pain to the mind like a cut is pain to the body. When someone is speaking what you know is truth and logic that goes against what you have come to believe and feel, you can shut the person out and even dehumanize them or keep listening and learning and considering their points. If your position is strong, it can stand up to another point of view. Through a desire to find an objective truth, you will learn to appreciate opposing information and enjoy having conversations with people who see things differently.

Practice repeating what someone said to you, ask them if it's accurate, and make sure you have their agreement before moving to making any counter points you have. Otherwise, you will both keep fighting to see who wins rather than make progress toward what is objectively correct. I used to do tech support and quickly realized that if I didn't understand someone well, I could be wasting time fixing a problem they did not have. But if I repeated back to them the point of their call and verified that I clearly understood, I was able to save both of us a lot of time and frustration.

Hate the idea, not the person. You can never change an idea, but if your idea is built on better logic and reason, it can stand against others. But remember to question your ideas and seek to understand when others challenge them. Keep an open mind about their own ideas. The more you learn about them, the more insight you will have for either changing yours or showing them why their idea has issues. Also, hate the idea but have compassion for why they think it. One surefire way to avoid slander or ad hominem attacks is to direct your argument toward the idea being presented rather than the person presenting it. You will always end up with a better argument and be able to leave the discussion with compassion and understanding for the person no matter how vile their idea may have been.

Remember that different viewpoints are an invitation to grow, not something to fear and avoid. We cannot grow when we are right.

Negotiated Transactions

All interactions, from talking to a cashier to an intimate relationship, are *negotiated* transactions. We choose what to offer and how we offer it as well as what we will and will not accept from the other people involved. What you accept from others is what you say you are worth, just like what you present to others is what you think they are worth. You also negotiate what you will accept from yourself. If it's okay to treat others a certain way, it's okay for you to be treated similarly.

There are some pre-negotiated aspects put in place by society that provide a great baseline for how to interact. This could mean small talk, how close to stand from another person, or the standards of what is and is not appropriate in polite society (usually best to keep your pants on and not talk with your food in your mouth). But if this becomes the primary track for an entire interaction, little will be accomplished. These standards are only meant as a starting point.

People say you shouldn't go deeper than small talk when first meeting someone. This is a horrible idea. When we think we are prisoners to what is acceptable, we must assume that others feel like they are in the same prison. People are dying to communicate and connect; that is who and what we are. Even if you don't agree with someone or they hate your opinion, an honest interaction means that you have both expressed yourself and been pulled out of your personal bubbles to get exposed to other ideas.

By speaking directly to a person from your heart, you become more of you and they can be more of themselves. You get from the system what you put into the system.

No Public Discussions on Social Media

Have more one-on-one conversations that are not online where everyone is trying to showboat and "virtue signal" (moral advocacy) for their side. Doing this creates more space for real honestly while allowing the other person to be themselves without showing off. There may still be "positions and postures" to navigate, but this is your best opportunity to meet soul to soul. This doesn't mean you will agree with them, but at least you can walk away with the pride of having done your best to be honest and trying to accept and understand the other person.

When you set a high standard for your personal actions, you are less accepting of low standards from those around you. As you come to expect more, you increase the quality of those you associate with and thereby make it easier for you to keep improving yourself.

Social media, on the other hand, has ruined our ability to be ourselves by making us afraid of showing who we really are for fear of being rejected. In social media discussions, the only strong opinions we express are usually tainted by what we think our group will "Like" us for saying rather than what is really in our minds or hearts.

Change Only Who You Can

Don't force change or insist upon change in others just because you think you are right. It will likely make them angry and you may be wrong or your methods may be flawed. Simply do what you think is right. You need not worry about what others do.

When a child, an employee, or even a pet has a "behavioral issue," I can beat my head against the wall trying to change them or make much better and smoother progress by changing my approach to them. I can only change me. When I change myself to the needs of the situation, I invite others to come with me.

I was once in a group where we went around a table pulling cards from a deck of "conversation starters." A card was pulled that asked what you would change about the world. People said honorable things like "I would make people more generous," "I would create world peace," and

"I would make people friendlier drivers." When the question got to me, I said I wouldn't change anything because I wouldn't want to force my will upon others. Sometimes we make the mistake of trying to control people, which infers that people need to be controlled and shouldn't be free to be themselves because otherwise they'd become rabid, murderous animals. Free will is what we have. If it is denied to anyone, we are telling ourselves that none of us deserve it.

Manipulating people has the same effect; if it's okay to manipulate others, you are telling yourself that it's okay for others to manipulate you.

When we try to force others to do something, we are seeking to impose our will on them which tells our subconscious that this is an acceptable behavior. Once it becomes acceptable, it makes it possible to push that line a little bit further so that one day I'm telling you to do this small thing and the next day I'm telling you how to live your life. And when we tell our subconscious that it's okay to impose our will on others, we will tend to allow others to force their will upon us. It's all the same to our subconscious no matter which direction it's going.

Whenever you feel you must force someone to do something, perhaps you haven't taken the time or had the patience to work through your ideas well enough to convince them that your way is better. This is interesting territory because I am not suggesting that you manipulate, bully, or guilt someone into doing something your way but find a different way to explain it to them so that they understand your point of view and your reasons for it. During such a process, you should also be open to hearing what they have to say because your way may *not* be the best way. If you have already examined your own beliefs and desires and made an honest effort to find the best solution or outcome, you should welcome someone questioning your ideas because your goal should always be to improve them or stay open to better ones.

The World Has Enough Victims

Don't tell people, either individually or in groups, that they are incapable of success without help or anything else that puts them into a mentally bad or insecure position. Any time you tell someone they are a victim, you reinforce their subconscious to assume they are less powerful than others. When you put all the blame on that other supposed oppressor, you remove the responsibility from the supposed victim and set them up for future failures. Someone being told that they are bad or hopeless means they may lose the drive to be the best version of themself and end up being that bad or hopeless person.

If someone raised a child and told them they were ugly or stupid all the time we would rightly see that as child abuse. Yet somehow telling a child they are oppressed and unable to succeed in the world, or that they are being held back is not considered abuse. To me, both are a form of abuse with the latter having the additional tragedy of setting a preloaded excuse for failure that could lead to someone never trying or never taking responsibility for the part they played in the failure. If one is not taking responsibility for the bad events and failures, they can never fully accept the pride of their accomplishments. To the subconscious we either have autonomy and power or it is in the hands of others. We must accept the bad as our doing to truly allow the successes to also be of our doing.

Telling people they have inherent road blocks, or they are bad, or even undeserving are self-fulfilling prophecies that you are imposing on them. By doing so, you make the world worse because you are demeaning the people around you, who influence who you are and who you think you can become. Remember we become like those we spend the most time around, so if we encourage their victimhood, we encourage our own through feedback and normalization.

Surrounding yourself with victims – with people you feel are weaker than you – makes it easier to justify giving up the hard work of your personal responsibility and the power that comes with it.

We point at our power. When you point at what is stopping you or holding you back, that is where your power is. What you just pointed at or blamed is what holds the power to further prevent you from succeeding or invite your success. Every tome your finger and blame point inward you become the reason for the failure and one with the power to overcome it. We either hold power over our lives or we do not. You cannot honestly, and in your heart, claim to have power over the good things in your life unless you also have power over the bad. The only way to have power over the bad things from happening again is to make them as much your fault as possible. If you are the cause of them, you are the one that can prevent them, if someone else is the cause of them, you must hope they will prevent them, the reliance and power is in their hands and they do not have a vested interest in your success. Remember, you can only change one person in this world.

If You Don't, I Won't Either

Here are a couple examples of where we try to get others to help us cover what we know to be an area of lack that we could be working on:

"Do I look fat in this?" I am asking because I know I do, but want you to tell me otherwise so I don't have to strive to be what I know I truly want to be.

"Did that help you?" I ask because I want you to tell me I did a good job so I do not have to feel obligated to work harder and I can leave with a false sense of accomplishment.

When we encourage growth in others, it will reverberate back and encourage growth within us. We also know that means work and effort on our part. This is why we accept when people are stuck; it gives us permission to accept our own stagnation, so we don't have to put in the effort to grow either.

A friend who genuinely cares about you will support your growth and likely be growing themselves so will want your honest encouragement. Someone who seeks to avoid the pain of growth will tell you that you are perfect just as you are. On the surface this seems kind, but in reality, it holds you down by removing your motivation and holds them down because they will see you as just like, perfect or not needing improvement.

"I need to lose 20 pounds" is met with either

"You look great the way you are. Don't conform to those beauty standards."

or

"You will feel amazing if you do, not just because you are lighter and healthier but to say you did it will feel wonderful!"

Take a close look at the people who say them. You will find those who say the first are avoiding feeling bad for not growing in an area of their life they don't want to acknowledge. Those who say the second may intimidate you if you want to improve but haven't given yourself permission to be the best version of you. But if you really want to lose 20 pounds, you want someone to say something encouraging that helps you along that path rather than, "You look fine."

Someone who cares about preserving their current state (which may be negative) will tell you that everything is okay, which means they are telling themselves that everything is okay. Think about why someone would say that. Because everything really *is* okay or so they don't have to make a change in their own lives and continue doing the same things they always have? If they're okay and you're okay, where is the motivation for growth?

Don't Go Down; Invite Them Up

We tend to lower ourselves to the lowest in the group far too often. When a person with a lower or more casual form of communication enters a group of well-spoken or well mannered people, you will see the entire group begin speaking or acting in this same manner rather than holding to their previously higher standards. This is a horrible thing to do to that person. You just told them, however unconsciously, that they aren't capable of the higher forms of communication and behavior you and the others enjoy. Perhaps they notice and assume you think them an idiot or somehow less intelligent. Whatever aspirations they may have had to improve in some way are likely diminished.

Whatever they think, everyone in the group has agreed that the person they are accommodating is of lower value. This is often a way that the shadow expresses itself. Your subconscious mind thinks of that person to be of lower value, but you haven't come to terms with why you think this or how it relates to you. In this case, your shadow will project that opinion through your lowered expectations of their abilities. As long as racism, sexism, classism, ageism, or whatever other-ism isn't dealt with in your shadow, you will continually do this type of thing to people you view as inferior. Even worse is that each time you act this way, you reinforce this in your shadow.

One way of dealing with this is to simply not act this way. See everyone as human and treat them as equal, which means they must be an equal. Don't expect everyone to be walking around with monocles and speaking as if they are at the queen's tea party, and don't raise or lower another's profile. You will either be insulting them or putting them on a pedestal.

Communication

"The fish trap exists to catch the fish. Once you've caught the fish, you can forget the trap. The rabbit snare exists to catch the rabbit. Once you've caught the rabbit, you can forget the snare. Words exist to convey meaning. Once you've caught the meaning, you can forget the words. Where can I find a man who has forgotten words, so I may have a word with him?"

—Chuang Tzu

The point of communicating is for ideas and concepts to be expressed to your audience and for them to understand that which is being expressed. There is a loss of happiness and comfort when we aren't being understood or when we do not understand. Happiness is replaced with confusion and frustration. When that flow of understanding is smooth, there is a sense of peace and contentment.

The Trouble with Words

A word attempts to relay a concept. It's the concept that's important, not the word. For example, if I am trying to convey a sense of peace and a calm mind, I might use the word "Satori." This works well if both you and I have the same understanding of satori and the feelings it brings up. But even though we may think we're in agreement, three communication issues can arise from this:

First, when I hear a word that is more complex, like a large word or one from a different culture, I pause while my brain processes the word into component parts such as definition, meaning, and feeling. For a moment, I am not with the speaker focusing on their intended point because parts of my brain are distracted trying to understand that word. A speaker wants an uninterrupted flow of understandable ideas, so consider your words when speaking. As a listener, be willing to ask for and agree on definitions.

Second, I often confuse "I know that word" with "I know that concept." Perhaps I read the definition of satori in a book and think I know what it means based on that definition and the surrounding context. This is great until we confront our lazy, energy-saving minds. Let's say I find myself speaking with someone who has spent years studying the concept of satori. They say that word and my brain kicks into lazy mode by assuming it already understands it so there is no need to use processing power to make sure I understand them. But do I really understand the word or its meaning? Consider what happens when you hear the word "enlightenment." To one person it may mean the end of a journey, while another may think of it as a step in their journey. Consider these two sentences: "I am enlightened." "I have been enlightened." They either mean the person has reached the end goal or taken a step forward, so the listener may not share the same understanding as the speaker.

Third, the ego. We get a sense of pride when we use more complex words or hear someone else say them and assume we understand. Once the ego is turned on and fed in this manner, it is hard to speak soul to soul or true self to true self. You are now speaking ego to ego. The speaker's ego is showing off all the fancy words it thinks it knows while the listener's ego is preparing to show how cool it is by projecting its familiarity with that word and any others. There might even be a competition over who can pronounce the word more ethnically correct. The winner must be more enlightened! It becomes a sparring match rather than two people embracing interesting ideas. I imagine the two egos giving each other high fives like gym bros: "We're killin' it, bro! Look at all these awesome words we remembered!" Meanwhile, the actual meaning is laying on the floor, bleeding out.

Speak Simply, so Others May Simply Understand

There is a difference between understanding a word or term and understanding the concept, especially when we use more complex words or words from other cultures. Both you and I can read the definition of *wu wei*, kundalini, satori, and cognitive dissonance, for example, and think we understand the word, but this is where the ego gets us in trouble, thinking it knows more than it does.

People notice when you use big or complex words; it slips right past them when you don't. Using easily understood words makes it harder for the ego to derail communication. There is less to latch on to. Smaller words slide by egotistical thought just like a poet, singer, or great speaker does. They are skilled in communicating a feeling or a concept to their listener and have learned to choose flow over ego.

It has been said that you understand a concept when you can explain it to a child. When we explain things to children, we don't think they're dumb, but we do use words and a form of speech that invite them to follow the idea rather than get stuck on the words. People pay closer attention to someone speaking in simple terms than someone who speaks in a more intellectual style. A great way to see this for yourself is to watch great public speakers; the more simply they speak; the more you feel pulled into their ideas.

Successful politicians are often good at this! (for better or worse)

Seek Common Ground

Healthy communication is especially difficult in modern-day politics, where divisiveness rules the day. Rather than make the extra effort to understand why another person thinks the way they do, we too often jump to the lazy and reactionary tactics of concluding, "Alt-right Nazis are incapable of loving other people" or "Godless lefties want to destroy society so they can get free stuff." Such simplistic and ignorant responses may help us conserve our mental energy by stopping us from really thinking about things, but they do little to help the world. You know in your heart the person you are talking to is not the evil demon you are lazily making them out to be. The truth is that once you start a real dialog with an open heart, you will realize just like yourself, people with different views also want the best for everyone and to make the world a better place. The world looks 1,000 times better and happier when we stop thinking that half of it is evil. With this awareness in mind, I approach others with a better attitude, which allows them to feel more secure and not defensive.

Know You Are Lazy

Lazy thinking also happens in the world of personal and spiritual growth. People will end a conversation by referring to something like "non-duality," "let go and let god," or "the science is final." These are all great concepts with immense value, but as conversation enders, they often come off as sounding like, "I have already spent some energy deciding which of these ideas I like best so no more thinking, listening, or understanding is needed."

The danger here is that you are allowing the thoughts of a previous and less experienced "you" define and make decisions for the new and improved you. This lazy thinking limits personal growth and ties us to ideas from a less aware and experienced person. Plus, open conversation allows people who may or may not agree to refine their ideas while bringing them into the light of scrutiny to see if they have validity and aren't just a lazy continuation of former thinking.

Our lazy minds also resist using additional energy for deeper consideration by choosing easy and familiar answers. Once we believe we have "thought something through," it's easy to conclude that no more thinking is necessary. Sadly, this limits our reality to what we like or what is easy. We should revisit our belief systems often to see if they are still what we align with. Most importantly, we should listen to others to test if we are being lazy in our thinking and to make sure we aren't ignoring other valuable perspectives. Remember: we can only grow when we are wrong.

However certain we are of our beliefs, there is something to be said about the glorious journey of sharing ideas with another person. This gives us a chance to see where we're in sync and where we can expand our understanding of the world and where we still have room to grow. Ideally, both sides will experience this growth, but if the conversation enders are thrown out, so is the conversation.

The key to inviting another person to be more open is to first be open and honest yourself, which requires that you are sincere about sharing your feelings and desires. This is another feedback loop. When I allow others to feel safe by expressing my authentic self, they will begin to open up and thus encourage me to be even more open.

Avoid Pointing at People

Point at things, not people. When you point at someone, it can feel accusatory and aggressive. But when you extend your hands with palms up and open and your fingers lightly extended, it feels like an invitation. If your intention is to let someone know that it's their turn to speak or to ask them what they want on their pizza, for example, try this simple gesture, as if you are welcoming and acknowledging them. Just making this small change will alter every conversation you have. Even if you are mad at someone, inviting them to connect in this way will help remove any tension since you are not putting them on the defensive or setting yourself up as an aggressor or predator they need to fear.

The same simple sentence can feel quite different and set the mood as happy and inviting or intense and aggressive depending on whether you point or gesture with a palm up open hand.

"What do you think?"

Pointing when saying this can put someone on the defensive. An open gesture feels much more invitational and encouraging.

Try this everywhere you go and especially in business meetings. The positive change in how people respond will improve their mood and that will feedback into improving yours as well. Now instead of dealing with people who feel on edge, you will be talking with people who feel they are being welcomed to participate.

Facial Expressions and Soul Language

As you learn to listen to your inner being through the practices shared at the beginning of the book, you will begin to better recognize the emotions of others as you speak with them. Part of the intent of those practices is to help you learn how to speak the language of souls – not just your own but others as well. It always helps me to know when something being discussed is making the other party happier or uncomfortable. Depending on the intent of the conversation or the type and level of the relationship, these signals can help determine if I should press on that point or move to another topic.

For example, because you are learning to recognize anger in yourself by how the muscles in the jaw and forehead feel tense, you can more easily see these signs in others. Perhaps the current topic is not to their liking or is something they wish hadn't come up. Perhaps you will notice them being intentionally deceptive by the small, creepy smile that happens when they think they are getting away with something, revealing what is called "duper's delight."

What is going on when someone's face suddenly looks 10 years younger? It may be accompanied by excited speech and body rapid movements. This is probably a topic they are passionate about and you could make their day by not interrupting and letting them have their moment. Just enjoy the bliss they are feeling and use that energy to make your own day brighter. You may also notice signs of awkwardness or embarrassment for their show of passion. This is your cue to encourage them by asking a question about the topic to get them back to feeling excited and validated. Their joy will feed your joy, so allow it for both your sakes.

Another way to encourage confidence in someone is to mimic them while they are speaking. If they lean forward as something gets more intense or interesting to them, you can do the same. When they smile or seem sad, follow along with those same expressions. Very often, we do this mimicking without intending to, but it can be done intentionally if you are trying to feel more connected to a conversation where the topic may be of less interest. The mimicking will help you stay more attentive to the speaker because the body is telling the mind that you are in sync and they are worth being interested in.

Is someone leaning away from you during the conversation or pointing their feet away? That's a good indication that, for whatever reason, they are done with the conversation. And feel free to notice this in yourself! If you are speaking to someone out of habit or perceived obligation, check to see if your body and feet are ready to leave. This is your right brain or your soul saying what your manners may not allow.

I don't want to make this too much about body language, because you will find through the intuitive practice of feeling your face and body that you automatically learn to read these signals. Over time, this language becomes more familiar and the vocabulary becomes more plentiful. If you want to learn about body language the traditional way, I highly recommend a book called *What Everybody Is Saying* by Joe Navarro. It's a personal favorite and easy to learn from – a great confidence booster that will help put feelings into words. I learned body language the traditional – from the outside in from observation – but later relied on learning from the inside by listening to my soul, which is where the practice I now teach came from.

Learning

"It is what we know already that often prevents us from learning."

–Claude Bernard

Our psychological shadow is cast upon people and things just as our physical shadow is. A physical shadow with a single point of light is very dark and defined. The more sources of light, the less dense and dark the shadow. The same holds true for our minds. Each psychological point of view we develop through knowledge, understanding, and compassion is another light source. The more light sources there are, the less dark and defined the shadow you cast upon others. You also make the world brighter for yourself by not casting dark shadows of your hidden aspects onto others. The more knowledge you have, the more, free, confident, and powerful you feel.

Compassion

Things that you do not understand will influence and guide you. If something causes you to feel hate, it has control over you. Learning compassion, by comparison, gives you control. You have power over it. Compassion and understanding are tied together just like ignorance and hate.

When we fear or hate something, we block ourselves from truly learning about it. When we are ignorant about something, we open ourselves to hating it or letting it become our fear. This cycle goes on until we choose to stop it by inserting love or knowledge.

Hate and fear are used in this world to control people. Someone who wishes to control you will do all they can to keep you ignorant. Someone who wants to empower you will encourage you to learn and understand everything, even (and especially) that which is outside of their bubble of beliefs.

You can control your car because you understand the steering wheel, shifter, and pedals. The more you know your car, the more control and power you have over it. Understanding how the engine and transmission work gives you knowledge for why and how the car moves and reacts to your actions. To someone who has never driven, sitting behind the wheel is intimidating and scary; the car controls them through that ignorance and fear. The same is true with other subjects including the people and groups we interact with. The better we understand them, the less likely our fear and the greater our control over our thoughts and emotions.

Knowledge and Compassion Are Equally Powerful

Increasing your compassion for someone will automatically allow you to better understand them, just as increasing your understanding will cause an increase in your compassion. I like to think of a monk who spends his days in a temple, rarely interacting with the outside world. And yet they are not afraid of the outside world because they start any encounter with compassion, which means they automatically have some understanding of what is in front of them.

You can tell a monk or priest how difficult your day was at your tech job and they don't need to know about the job or the tech to understand you. Because they have compassion for you, they "get" your issues and the feelings you have about your life. I've spent a lot of time in tech, so when someone speaks to me of the troubles or joys in that job, I understand it, so having compassion for them is easy. It goes either way just as easily.

The deeper you understand someone or something, the more compassion you will have. You may strongly dislike a thief, but once you understand how their life brought them to that point, you can have compassion for them. You don't have to accept their behaviors or open yourself up to being taken advantage of, but you can understand why they think stealing is okay or necessary and have compassion for how and why they are ruining their lives. Perhaps a liar has low self-esteem or a fear that causes them to lie. I don't have to enable them or accept them into my life to have compassion for why they behave that way.

Understanding what it must be like for someone to have so much hate that they feel the need to hurt or kill someone leads to having compassion for what a terrible world that must be to live in. Imagine how they will feel if they decide to "confront" their action or simply grow old living with the memory of committing a violent act. We can also have compassion because we understand what it's like to outgrow our past or come from a bad place. The more I understand how people limit themselves, the less I hate them and the more I feel compassion for being stuck in beliefs that no longer serve their best interests or their soul's purpose.

I was at the gym one day and witnessed a man being very rude and unnecessarily abusive to someone who worked there. Stepping in was not necessary as the employee handled it most admirably. I realized from watching that interaction that I could have compassion for that man. While the employee and I were only in his negative presence for a moment, he has to live with that person he is all the time.

The feedback loop he kept himself in was absolutely terrible. He would treat others rudely, and no doubt could sense they did not like him because of it. Their obvious contempt justified to him that treating them rudely was appropriate, which then caused people to like him less. Perhaps he desired the feeling of power he had over others who were forced to be polite no matter his ill behavior, but still that is a feedback loop of loneliness from everyone being beneath him, all this to prop himself up artificially. I have great compassion for how miserable and soul destroying that must be. I am under no obligation to befriend him or try to fix him. What I can do is allow my world to be happier by having compassion and understanding over contempt that I take away with me to color my world and subsequent interactions.

Be brave and take the first step to normalize understanding and compassion toward those you don't like. Be open to starting an honest conversation with them. It will change how you see them, even if at the end of the conversation they are not a candidate to become a new friend. At the very least, they become a source of new understanding. Taking such a risk will also normalize it for them to have more understanding and compassion for you.

Your Heart Is Telling You

Learning to listen to your true self will help you know when you are stopping short of a more ultimate truth or a necessary change in beliefs. Are all of your beliefs truly aligned with your inner being or do some of them just feel comfortable? Do you avoid learning about a topic because it might conflict with a belief about it and the idea of doing so causes fear or discomfort? Why would you be afraid of knowledge? Go where your mind does not want you to go; that is where your evolution is. When you are scrolling on the internet, go back and look at what you ignored and rushed past. Did you avoid reading that article or watching that video because you "didn't want to go there"? The things we run from and ignore are usually the ones we most need to experience for our growth. We can only grow when we are wrong, one who is always correct stays the same. It is better to be open to being wrong than to remain stagnant.

Dig into something new or, even better, closely examine a long-held belief. Ask deep-dive questions and keep going even when you think you have an answer. Ask questions beyond your comfort zone. We often stop asking questions when we find an answer we like. When you like an answer, question why you like it. Stopping where it's comfortable allows our ego and our fears to control what we should or shouldn't think or be interested in. Even (or especially) when you come upon an ultimate truth, I would invite you to ask why you think it's an ultimate truth and why you aren't delving deeper.

When someone mentions fly fishing, astronomy, golf, knitting, biology, roller derby, or some other topic you have no knowledge of, take a few minutes to learn something about it. We live in an amazing time where everything is at our fingertips. I don't have to drive to the library to learn about something; I can look it up right on my phone or computer. In just 15 minutes, you can gain enough basic knowledge to understand and appreciate almost any topic an "expert" may be trying to explain. Added bonus: You might get lucky when playing trivia!

You also may find something new to love that you never would have imagined. Opening yourself up to growth in this way makes self-improvement a habit that expands to other areas of your learning and life. The world is more beautiful when we meaningfully connect with others instead of thinking of them as "those people."

Yes, we need to pay bills, but why make the experience of going to work a miserable one? If you have a long commute, get audio books or listen to podcasts that expand your knowledge. If you talk to people all day, make it a challenge to see how many you can get to smile from a kind word. Exercise compassion for the jerks you deal with because you are probably happier at your core than they are.

Nice Bubble You Got There

Our assumptions about the world make us feel safe because we know where the line is between our personal sainthood and the "evil people over there." But you know what they say about assumptions: They make an "ass" out of "u" and "me." So, I again invite you to expand your knowledge. Instead of learning about something that reinforces your current beliefs, open your mind to learning about that with which you disagree. If you are religious, ask an atheist friend for a video or an article that makes their point. If you are the atheist, ask a religious friend for something that explains their beliefs. If you fall on the political left or right, honestly ask and seek to learn why they believe as they do, maybe truly knowing why they believe as they do will reveal something about one or both of you. There is something powerful about asking someone for their opinion or point of view. You set them up to be a teacher and prime yourself for learning without either of you being defensive or becoming an aggressor. This willful and intentional act of seeking lowers the defenses of the ego. It tells the ego, I am seeking this, so allow the information to be ingested and considered. When information is brought to you the ego has those castle defenses up, when you seek you are lowering the drawbridge and inviting it in.

I have been religious, atheist, and spiritual in my life at different times. Presently I have landed on a spiritual way of thinking and being as what fits my soul currently. I mention this to help relay something that drove me from the atheist and materialist way of thinking. It was learning that we still do not know where consciousness comes from. That point of view still requires magic but denies that it does. From the materialist and non-spiritual perspective, it is assumed that our consciousness comes from all the food we have eaten but not yet pooped out. One could easily say there is magic involved with chewing and swallowing food, then having consciousness suddenly arise from it. I mention this not to steer one toward spirituality so much as an invitation to consider your current beliefs and find the holes in your own thinking to see if you can yourself spot them without them being pointed out to you. It is a fun, rewarding, and challenging exercise.

If your ideas are aligned with your true self, they will hold up to this new information. Maybe you will find your truth somewhere in the middle or you embrace the new information and completely change your mind. Maybe after listening to and understanding them, you will be the one who gets asked to share your point of view and you end up helping someone understand you, so they can now have a better view of *your* morals. By normalizing the act of listening and understanding, you too will be heard and understood.

This is far a different strategy than arguing with someone, our natural inclination is to make something into an argument and then try and win, to convince the other person to come to our side. When we choose instead to seek out new information, we're doing it not from our ego but from a more open mindset. My goal is understanding, not winning. I'm willing to analyze new information and come to my own conclusion.

There is no risk with such an approach. Worst-case scenario is a better understanding of why the other person/group thinks the way they do. It may not be evil or stupid but simply different. It has been my experience that most of us want the best for the world and the people in it, even the people I think are completely off their rockers. Yes, there are a few out there who are truly bad, but they are a small percentage and rarely encountered. Let me say that again, they are very rare and most likely they are not the person you are speaking with; they are extremely rare to encounter.

In today's world of social media everyone wants to show other people who are watching the comment thread how amazing they are and how good they are at knocking the other person down. But really, that's not what it's about or shouldn't be what it's about. It should be about learning and about bringing the best idea to the forefront, that best idea may not be your idea. To know if the person you are speaking with in any open forum, online or in a group of people, is interested in truth or if their goal is virtue signaling what they think will win points with their group, ask them to move the conversation to a more private forum where both can express ideas without fear of or pandering to the observing mob. I have found most will decline because they do not seek truth, but the few that do will be great for mutual teaching and understanding.

The most effective and legitimate criticisms can only be made about something of which you have solid knowledge as opposed to assumptions and biases. I can criticize people on the political left because I used to be there, but when I was on the left and criticized those in opposition, I didn't know enough to do a good job. My criticisms were shallow. Now that I have spent more time understanding centrist, libertarian, and right-wing perspectives, I feel confident giving valid criticisms of them as well as those of the left. They all have their dogmas, logical fallacies, and inconsistencies. I now can see more clearly which ideas and ideologies to respect and which ones are inaccurate or mislead. I also gained compassion for those with whom I disagreed, but I first had to independently and honestly study all with an open mind and heart. The best insights came not from telling people what I think but from asking them what they think and making an honest effort to understand their response.

It's important to find the good in what we dislike and the bad in what we like. If we only see or speak about the good on "our side," we have made a steel man. When we only see the bad on the "other side," we have made an easy to knock over straw man. This is how we know we aren't dealing with reality; we are loving and hating mere icons or avatars rather than reality itself. Consider this with politicians, policies, cultures, ideologies, religions, science, spirituality, or anything else where you find yourself thinking or speaking in extremes.

When you look into "the opposition's" information, you likely spot the manipulative language being used. When you look at your own frame of reference, that manipulative language may be harder to see but does exist in your groups as well. Our instinct tells us to claim a superiority of ideas, that "those people" are fooled and indoctrinated but my side is immune, but history tells us to be very careful with that line of thinking. It's important to see the manipulation being used on both sides in order to uncover the highest truths. Seeing it in your groups and beliefs is the most useful to your growth.

We tend to ask the wrong questions: "Am I being manipulated or controlled?" "Am I in an echo chamber?" Your ego will deny the validity of these before you even get to the end of the question. That is what the ego does. The faster you deny, though, the more suspicious you should be of your certainty. More to the point: You need to ask better questions that come from assuming that you *are* being controlled and in an echo chamber. So the better questions are, "*How* am I being controlled?", "What was I indoctrinated into?", and "*In what ways* am I in an echo chamber?"

If you want only a single point of confidence and power, then you can stay in your echo chamber and learn everything there is to know about that one topic, point of view, or side. But if you want to feel more broadly and legitimately confident and powerful, seek knowledge about things you don't understand or find disagreeable. Learn about why they are, what they are, and how they work. If you still find them disagreeable, at least now you have the right information to take them on.

Chains of Friendship

Have you ever hesitated to watch, read, or listen to something that goes against your beliefs or what you want to be true? Are your options to learn being limited by your groups or your own habits and biases? Our minds are lazy and will often resist going against the crowd or thinking about a subject beyond its surface. Your ego and lazy mind say, "I've already thought about that and formed my opinion, so I don't need to process it further." But which you came to that conclusion? An old version of you? A scared you? Maybe you were under some type of emotional influence when you formed your opinion on that matter. It might be time to think again. It's your mind and you have permission to revisit and investigate anything you desire.

Speaking of revisiting, if you use social media this trick is easier, but you can also do it by remembering what was said in a conversation that you passed over and did not address. On social media we have the benefit of it all being laid out for us. As you scroll your media feed for a bit, stop, go back.

Look at everything you scrolled past that you did not look into. Take a moment to ask yourself honestly why you did not read a particular article or watch that video. Did you assume you already knew what it would say, or did you think it was from "those people" and probably just lies or propaganda? Is your mind strong enough to investigate and consider any information to see if it has value? Do you think others are being tricked but you are immune? Are you and your group superior to others? Sounds a bit dangerous to think of it in those terms, doesn't it? Try going back and understanding the info you scrolled past or ignored, see it as trying to come together instead of making enemies you can later justify atrocities against as history has shown us we all have the unfortunate capacity to do.

I felt happier and freer when I let myself out of my echo chamber. What image comes to mind when you think of an echo chamber? A cave or a box, right? That doesn't seem very free. The first step, then, is to honestly decide if you are in one. You may not think so at first because you feel confident in what you know, but what do you know? Clips and memes provided by others in your echo chamber? What about something you hear from outside the chamber? Is your first reaction to battle the person who said it? Or do you honestly and openly consider what someone else is saying with the intention to understand them better?

When we make the choice to look at something from the point of view of another, it's different than when someone else tells us to do it or asks us to change our mind based on what they've said. The best results for me have come when I make up my own mind without influence from my ego or the egos of others. When we allow ourselves to choose what we want to learn, no information is bad information.

But what if I change my mind and my friends no longer like me? This will tell you a lot about those "friends," right? I spent a lot of time building friendships only to have them reveal that I was not a friend but a pawn to their cause. Once I got "out of line" and started thinking differently, I was no longer the good and helpful buddy, but the enemy. Looking back, I'm grateful I was exiled from those groups of people. I likely would have kept them as my "handlers" telling me what to do and how to behave had they not pushed me away. Staying could have stopped or limited my learning and growth as a person. It sucked at the time to lose those friends, but in the process I learned who I was and that I can leave people who hold me back because I will find other more compatible people to replace them – and repeat as necessary. This is not to say that people are disposable; they are indeed valuable. But by staying with those not also choosing to be wrong and grow as individuals, I am sabotaging my own further growth. There is a big difference between leaving someone behind by stepping on them or pushing them away and leaving because someone declined your invitation to grow with you. It's not about finding 'better' people but *more compatible* people.

Closing Smiles

"I love those who can smile in trouble."

— Leonardo da Vinci

Be the Butterfly Wings that Put the Wind in Someone's Sails

These interconnected systems along with our good intentions can work miracles in the world, or at least in someone's world. A small act from you to someone else can be just the thing they need to turn from sad and frustrated to hopeful and energetic. When I take a moment to tell someone I appreciate them or something they are working on, I give myself a reward and give them at least a smile. But it can be so much more than a smile. Imagine someone working on a project with passion and purpose but who are feeling a little frustrated with it. Maybe it's not seen as valuable by others or they've hit a wall and don't know how to get past it. Perhaps they are close to quitting and throwing it all away. Then comes the angel they didn't know they were waiting for. Taking a few minutes to see and appreciate what they are working on can put breath back in their lungs and wind in their sails. Maybe you actually love it

243

and your kind words give them the fuel to keep going for the one more day needed for it to take off.

This can apply to someone having a bad day/week/year — just noticing them and asking how they are doing sets them on an upward spiral. I realized how often I would walk around with a frown and make worlds darker by doing so. I felt shame and regret for missing those opportunities, and I've used those feelings to remind me I could do better. Now I do my best to smile no matter where I am and feel a great sense of pride imagining I might have helped each person I encountered. I could have been that little flap of butterfly wings that powered them on a journey around the world. You, too, can feel that lift with just the tiniest of steps. It will cost you nothing but might give you and others everything.

Make Yourself Happier by Making Yourself Happier

When I talk in this book about how thoughts and actions both positive and negative loop through our circles and feed back to us, this is the system I invite you to consider. We influence those around us just as they do us. We cannot control what they do and shouldn't want or need to; we just need to change ourselves and watch the magic happen. We get back from these circles and systems what we put into them. This is how we will make ourselves happier: by actually making ourselves happier.

We tend to forget how connected we are with everyone else and how each part of the system needs the other parts. Appreciate the different systems you are part of, how they affect you, and what you can learn from them. Insert just a little more positivity into them – for everyone's sake!

You Should Smile More!

It is often thought of as offensive when someone says to smile more. This is silly, we should take it as a kind reminder the person has given us. We can thank them for noticing we have not been putting that extra little bit of joy into the world. Who cares whether their intent for you to smile was admirable or not, they have still done you a favor. Besides, if you were already smiling they would not have said it in the first place. What benefit does it provide to you or the world for you to get angry that someone told you to smile? It's like I said about getting offended, you are mad because someone else noticed the problem before you did. Now you must either give them credit and be grateful, or get angry. Only one of those choices makes your world a brighter place.

HIHO

Do your best to remember to keep a subtle smile on your face as you go through the day. Notice how it affects your mood. I do this as much as possible, softly smiling without intent at a flower, a box of cereal, a dog, someone who is annoying me – anything and everything. It makes the world feel happier and softer. When you encounter others, no matter the situation, keep the same subtle smile for the cute guy, the angry person, the store clerk, a coworker, and especially someone you don't get along with very well. You will find that people react very positively to a smile even if it's barely perceptible. They may smile back at you or at someone else who then smiles at someone else and the contentment spreads like a virus in a positive feedback loop. Imagine how you feel when encountering a monk walking at peace with everything around them. Try to mimic that, just subtly smile and find something to appreciate about everything you encounter. When you notice you forgot to carry that smile, smile at how wonderful it is you remembered.

The more you smile the better you feel, the better you feel the easier it is to smile more. This is the easiest happiness feedback loop you can intentionally create and feed!

"or Smile"

My logo and signature are constant reminders to myself and others that no matter what it can be made better with a smile.

Ever catch yourself walking around with a grumpy face. Don't be mad at yourself for doing it; maybe even see how funny it is and use that humor to replace it with a smile. How does it feel to walk past someone with an angry face compared to someone who is smiling and seems at peace? When someone has a pleasant smile, you can feel that happiness. Wouldn't you feel great if you produced this feeling of joy in those who walk past you? Seeing those who walk past you catch that smile allows you to see more smiles and makes smiling easier. Pretty soon the world goes from gloomy to beautiful. It is the feeling that we live in an ugly world that keeps us feeling locked into unhappiness, but by inserting our light, we make the world better for ourselves and others.

Have sympathy for those who are angry or lash out. You don't have to accept their behavior, and if it's safe to do so, call them out on it. The important thing to remember is that at some point you will walk away from them while they remain stuck in that feeling. You want to avoid inserting someone else's negativity into your feedback loop. Instead, let it go and replace it with compassion and a smile. After all they have to live with themselves being unhappy all the time, while you can live with yourself in ever increasing joy and contentment.

And remember to put a little smile under the word "or" every now and then to remind yourself that even a little positive influence in your day can snowball into another amazing year.

I could _____, "or smile"...